From Base Camp
To Summit

Contents

Introduction by the Chairman of the 2003 Convention

Keswick 2003 certainly set records. Numbers, while I'm not sure they were a record, were extremely encouraging. During the second week a small extra tent had to be hired to contain the numbers.

Surely the temperatures in the first week were a record! Well over 100 degrees was reached inside the tent on a number of occasions. Sales of bottled water were impressive!

The theme of discipleship was felt by many to be extremely appropriate at this time in our church and nation. Many are making professions of faith in Christ through for example, Alpha and Christianity Explored courses. The ministry of the Convention addressed the issues of being established in Christ and growing in our knowledge and following of Him. Testimonies of God's blessing through this ministry were expressed to me throughout the Convention and written testimonies continue to be sent. We give thanks to God and trust that the published ministry will also lead to the blessing of many people.

So we look forward to next year and particularly to addressing the vital theme of the sovereignty of God. The title for the Convention will be "Out of Control – the Sovereignty of God in a World of Uncertainty". See you there.

Your brother in Christ
Peter Maiden

Editor's Introduction

Summer 2003 saw another three week Convention and another struggle to decide what to include in the Year Book! This volume contains many of the evening addresses but also two 'firsts' – Steve Chalke's seminar on how to get involved in your local community and Steve Bell's lecture, 'A Grace Response to Muslims'. It was felt that both of these contained such excellent material that we had to use them.

A word to any purists – no attempts have been made to change the style of any of the preachers – this book aims to be an accurate record of Keswick 2003, and to do that we need to capture a little of what it was like to sit and listen, first in the blazing sunshine and then with rain hammering on the tent, to some superb and challenging teaching. Working on this material is always a joy – this year it has been a lifeline.

Enjoy!

Ali Hull
October 2003

The Bible Readings

The Centrality of Christ

by Joseph Stowell

JOSEPH STOWELL

A graduate of Cedarville College, (Ohio), and Dallas Theological Seminary, Dr Stowell has pastored churches for sixteen years, the most recent being the Highland Park Baptist church of Southfield, Michigan – a church of more than one thousand eight hundred, with a Christian school of seven hundred and fifty students. Dr Stowell became the seventh president of the Moody Bible Institute in 1987. He oversees the entire scope of MBI's ministries – education, broadcasting, publishing and church/conference ministries. In addition to these responsibilities, he reaches many through 'Proclaim!', a daily broadcast put out on more than two hundred and fifty stations. In addition to his pastoral work, Dr Stowell is active in international missions and has authored more than ten books, including *Strength for the journey*, *Simply Jesus* and *The Trouble with Jesus*. He is married to Martie and they have three children and seven grandchildren.

Chapter 1
The reflection of the ultimate glory of God

Introduction

Maybe we ought to start by just setting some ground rules. Number one is that this is all about you; not somebody you know. Rule number two is you can't shout 'Amen!' on something you want somebody else to get. Rule number three, and this is by far the most important: you need to be here with a heart that is ready to hear from God. I am but a middle man in a divine transaction between you and God. I hope I disappear and that you hear from God.

I want to tell you what kind of people need to listen this week. First of all, those of you who tend to live on the grumpy side of life desperately need what God's going to teach you. Those of us who are long on mad and short on mercy will need this. Those of us who view our Christianity as being something that's all about the rules and the more rules we keep the better we are... You need this. Those of you who are tired of guys like me talking about grace and love and mercy: you need this. If you read the headlines about AIDS and how it's destroying Africa, if you walk down the streets and see the homeless, if you read stories about the impoverished sections of the cities of our world, and if they're only headlines to you and they don't tug at your heart, then you need what God's going to teach you this week. If you're stuck in a world of past defences and most of your life is about going back and thinking about it over and over again; if you have been robbed of a future because you're always in the past, then may God speak to your heart and liberate your life.

Be like Jesus

The theme this week is discipleship, seeing Jesus in a fresh light and following his example and becoming fully devoted followers of Jesus Christ. When I was thinking about that, it seemed to me that there was only one place we could really go if we want to make it succinct, and that was to the Gospel of John. The theme text is going to be John chapter 1 verses 14 through 18. I want you to keep in mind this call of Christ for you to become a follower of him. How do you glorify God? By becoming like Christ, for he was the glory of God. The touch point of the glory of God, for us, is to become more and more like Christ all the time. That's your redemptive purpose. Some of you are going to say, 'I can't get my arms around that project, it's too challenging, I'll never get there.' Let me help you: John 1:14

> And the word become flesh and dwelt among us, and we beheld his glory, the glory as of the only one begotten of the Father, full of grace and truth. John bore witness of him and cried out, saying, 'This was he of whom I said "he who comes after me has a higher rank than I, for he existed before me."' For of his fullness, we have all received and it has been grace upon grace for us. For the law was given through Moses but grace and truth were experienced through Jesus Christ. No man has seen God at any time, the only begotten Son, who is in the bosom of the father, he has explained him.

This week, it's my prayer that we will get a biblical grip on the reality of the fullness of the reliable grace of God. Not only in our lives, but to be like Christ by extending it to others.

John defines Christ's likeness in a very succinct way, doesn't he? I like to think someone gave John this project: 'You've lived with Jesus for three years, 24/7. Could you describe him in twenty five words or less?' John takes twenty-eight words to do it. John said 'I knew him intimately and at the end of all that what really impresses me about Jesus is that he was the fullness of grace and truth.' That is the summary statement of Jesus.

If I'm determined, by God's grace, under the power of the Holy Spirit, to become like Christ, that needs to be the summary statement of my life. What's important for us, if we are to be disciples marked by the reality of Jesus, is to unwrap this thing of grace and truth and to use it as a benchmark in our own lives. For when we make progress here, then we know the joy of bringing glory to God by being like Christ.

What does this mean? For years I have thought this is about the Lord's soft side and hard side all combined; that he is grace, the soft, warm merciful kindness of Jesus, but he is also about truth. Jesus was the truth and he is the truth and he talked the truth. Sometimes his truth is so in the face of the crowd, that it was too much for people to bear and they walked away. Jesus was both grace and truth. However, I found it interesting the more I studied this target for my life that I came to realise John is not talking about the soft side/hard side of Jesus here.

I don't want to take away anything you've had your whole life, or sermons you've preached, but I had to take away my own sermons that I'd preached, as I began to look at this. Because the word for truth in the Greek is not always about propositional truth. It also means true in the sense of authentic, faithfulness, reliability, something you can count on, the real deal. Could it be that John had that in mind? That Jesus was full of grace and faithfulness and authenticity and reality? Like you say to yourself, 'I need to be true to myself.' That doesn't mean you stand in front of the mirror and spew out propositional truth. What that means is you need to be true to your word, a reliable person. And, since the Greek could go both ways, I find myself wondering could it be that John is saying that when he experienced Jesus, that Jesus was full of grace and faithfulness? That the grace of Jesus was a reliable grace, that you could count on him to be the fullness of grace.

The glory of God

Before we read that he is the fullness of grace and truth, John talks about the glory of God. We read, 'And the word became flesh and dwelt among us and we beheld his glory', and it was like the glory of the Father. This is the first initial imprint of John's affirmation of the divinity of Jesus Christ. He's saying I beheld something in him and it was the glory as of the only begotten of the Father. What is the glory of God? Hang on to that just a minute.

Not only do we have that but we also have, in this context, the law given to Moses; verse 16. We read 'of his fullness ... we have all received . . . grace upon grace ... For the law...' So we have the law and then we have Moses. And then in verse 18 we have 'no man has seen the Lord at any time' unless you have seen Jesus. Jesus has revealed him and so you have four elements wrapping the context; the glory of God, the law, Moses, and an unseen God that Jesus has revealed.

You need to know that John and all of the New Testament writers wrote out of the context of the Old Testament. They did not have the New Testament but they were well versed in the major moments of the Old Testament. I ask myself, what sort of allusion do we have here to the glory of God, the law of Moses and the unseen God? My mind races immediately to Exodus 33 and 34. The context for Exodus 33 and 34 is that Moses has been called up to Mount Sinai. He's there too long for the patience of the Israelites, so they recruit Aaron to relapse back to the paganism of Egypt. They give all their gifts and they melt them down and make a calf. They are actually having an orgy at the bottom of Mount Sinai.

While Moses was up on Mount Sinai, God has told him to carve two tablets of stone. Here we have Moses, and the law. God has written the law and then Moses comes down and he hears the music. It reminds him of the orgies of Egypt. Then he sees and he is so distraught that he takes the two tablets of stone and crashes them down and they are split apart. He goes back up the mountain pleading with God and he says to God (33:13) 'now therefore I pray thee, if I have found favour in thy sight, let me know thy ways'. Verse 18; Moses pleaded with God, 'I pray thee, show me thy glory.'

Here we have all the elements of John 1:14 through 18 coming together. You've got the glory of God, the law and Moses and you have the unseen God. Later on when God reveals his glory to Moses, he says to Moses you cannot see me so I will hide you in the cleft of the rock and then I will walk past you and I will reveal my glory to you. It seems to me this is exactly what John has in mind. If you were to ask God to reveal to you his glory in one statement, what do you expect he might reveal to you; especially with Israel violating and deeply offending the almighty God at the bottom of Mount Sinai? What would you expect God to do? I would expect God to reveal his holiness and the terror of his wrath. Did these people deserve annihilation at the bottom of that mountain? Absolutely. But this is the bit that shocks me and when I saw this, my heart was riveted.

> Moses rose up early in the morning and he went up to Mount Sinai as God had commanded him. He took two stone tablets in his hand and the Lord descended in the cloud and stood there with him, and he called upon the name of the Lord. Then the Lord passed by in front of him and proclaimed 'The Lord, the Lord God, compassionate and gracious, slow to anger and abounding in loving kindness and truth.'

Just hang on to that for a minute, OK?

Verse 7: God says 'I am the God who keeps loving kindness for thousands, who forgives iniquity, transgression and sin'. And then he turns and says 'Yet I will by no means leave the guilty unpunished.' You say 'I like that part; if I'm going to be like Jesus and glorify God, you can have the grace stuff and I'm going after my enemies.' I just want to remind you of Romans chapter 12. Paul says in verse 17, 'As much as it is possible with you live in peace with all men, do not repay evil with evil but put wrath in its proper place. For God says

"Vengeance is mine. I will repay" says the Lord.' It is his business to deal with our enemies. Every time you and I try to deal with our enemies, and are vengeful, we always get messed up, don't we? We get entangled in this quagmire of broken relationships. And the reason is God didn't give you the grace to do that, is it's not in your job description. Please quit trying to do what God is supposed to do!

The God of compassion

Now I want to go back to that phrase I told you to hang onto. God says he is the God of compassion, gracious and willing and ready to forgive. Then he called himself a God of loving kindness and faithfulness. Now are you thinking about John 1:14? The whole context of the glory of God, of the law and Moses, of the unseen God: John has this in mind. I'll tell you why I think John has this in mind. This little formula, 'I am a God of love, kindness and truthfulness' is the lead statement of God throughout the whole Old Testament. It is what God wants to be known by. Let's take the two Hebrew words: the words 'loving kindness' are the Hebrew word *hesed*. It means loyal love, love regardless, the action of kindness as a covenant commitment of God to his people. It is the lead quality of God revealed in the Old Testament but it is always connected in this phrase with the Hebrew word *emit*, which can be translated 'truth' or more accurately 'faithfulness'. In other words, 'I'm a God of loyal love but I'm not fickle; I'm true to my loyal love. You can count on me to loyally love you, period.' That's what God wanted us to know about him, and that's exactly why God repeats this Old Testament formula in John 1:14, when John says 'I spent three years with Jesus. He's just like God, he claimed he was God. Was he like the God I learned about in Rabbi school, full of reliable grace and faithfulness? He was, so when he told me he was God, I believed him. I'd never met anyone like this before; the fullness of grace that is reliable and faithful.'

A lot of your neighbours – and the people you work with – think that the Old Testament is about the mad side of God; God in his fighting gear, who kills people and makes war and then finally the New

Testament came and Jesus arrives, and he brought in this wonderful grace. That is such a non-biblical thought. There is no formula describing God, more frequently used in the Old Testament, than this *hesed/emit* formula. It's what God is trying to get across.

Jonah

Jonah, the chief prophet in Israel – God comes to him and says go to Nineveh and proclaim their sin against them. Jonah, the good guy, he doesn't even think about it. He just says 'I'm not doing it.' You might say, 'Why did Jonah refuse to go to Nineveh?' If you read the book of Jonah, you see that their major sin was their violence. God said 'I can no longer tolerate it and you must repent of it or I will judge you.' They were the military might of the day, they were the main threat to Israel; maybe that's why Jonah didn't want to go. But my first guess is that he's scared of going to a place like that. They'd conquer their enemies and behead the whole enemy army and all the way back to Nineveh they'd build pyramids of these heads to celebrate the victory. Jonah, this little Jewish prophet with his robe and his long white beard and Torah tucked under his arm, going, 'You guys are sinners.' Boy, that guy is, like we say back in America, he's toast. He's saying to God, 'I'm not going to be a skin on a wall. I'm out of here.'

He runs from God and as he runs from God, God sends this storm. By the way, in Jonah chapter one, everything's obeying God, except the prophet; the wind, the sea, the fish… and he's sound asleep in the midst of the storm. So for all us lame brain Christians who think, 'I have a real peace about this, it must be the will of God…', he was radically rebellious and he had so much peace. Your rationalisation and your excuses can actually give you a false sense of peace.

He's sound asleep in the middle of the storm and the captain comes down and wakes him up. They were dicing on the decks to see who was at fault and even the dice obey God. They ask Jonah 'Who are you?' and he has to give a testimony. He says, 'I am from Israel and I worship the God of the sky and the sea. It's my fault.' You might think that Jonah, at this point, might say 'Here's the remedy, let me repent and put me off at the next stop. I'll go to Nineveh' and the sea would be stilled. But Jonah doesn't say that. Jonah says, 'Throw me overboard.' He is saying 'I would rather die than obey God. I'd rather die than go to Nineveh.'

God says 'Boy, did he wreck the plan. I got to start all over again. We'll have to wait another twenty years whilst I get myself another prophet.' No, you see, God's a lot like the Royal Canadian Mounted police – they always get their men. God is like the hound of heaven, he will pursue you in your disobedience because he loves you and he has a bigger plan. So he says to the fish 'See? Lunch!' And Jonah spends three days and three nights in a sleazy underwater hotel before he finally says 'I give in.' That's how stubborn he was about this and he goes and preaches and Nineveh repents. You would have thought that he would have been just thrilled. This is prayer letter material, isn't it? 'Thanks for your investment in me this month. I just led Nineveh back to the Lord and reduced the threat against Israel.' I mean his support is going to go through the skies!

He is sitting, chapter 4, outside the city of Nineveh, mad at God for giving up his judgement on Nineveh. And he tells us why he didn't go and it has nothing to do with being afraid. Listen to his words. 'Do you want to know, Lord, why I didn't want to come here?' – for all of you who think that the Old Testament is about God's mad side – 'because I knew that thou art a gracious and compassionate God, willing to forgive.' I knew that about you. Everybody in the Old Testament knew that that was God's leading glory, the leading characteristic of God – he is a compassionate God, who is willing to forgive even the worst of offences.

Jonah, the best guy in town, refused to be the middleman in a grace transaction between God and his worst enemies. Just let that sink in. I think preachers ought to stop preaching every once in a while and let the Spirit knock some things in. Jonah refused to be a middleman in what God wanted to be a dynamic, life-changing grace transaction between God and the enemies of Jonah. I wonder how often in your life, and how often in my own life, God has asked me to extend his marvellous grace to an undeserving person, and I've said 'No way. I refuse to be the middleman in a grace transaction here.'

If you count yourself amongst those types of people, a
have to do, then we desperately need to hear what we'r
about this week. Jesus was known first and foremost by
grace, regardless. He was known by extreme grace all the
cross and if we want to be like him, then we must be kno
as well.

What is grace?

Definitions are very important, aren't they? Grace gets t
church word. We sing about it but you have to know
Your life is driven by the definitions. It's like the Texa
was over here in the UK, doing some agriculture con
to the UK farmer, 'How big's your place here?' And th
'Maybe a mile by a mile, it's not real big.' And he s
rancher, 'How big's your place, back in Texas?' 'H
says. 'It's hard to tell you, it's so big. Maybe I can tell
in my truck in the morning when the sun comes up
long, by the time the sun goes down I'm still on m
farmer says 'Oh, I had a truck like that once myself
All of that to make you understand that you nee
inition of grace. The definition is unmerited favo
definition. Nobody's asking 'Yes, but what does th
satisfied with the technical, theological term. Let's
bit. As we've studied here in Exodus, if you go b
God reveals his glory, (before he said 'I'm a Go
kindness') he says 'I'm a God of compassion. I'
cious, I'm a God who is willing to forgive.' Ever
that we can understand some of the specifics of
extrapolation of unmerited favour for you, that
its reflection of the glory of God in his grace,
Christ. It is the action of abundant kindness,
most undeserving offenders. It is the action of
kindness, regardless of any circumstance. The
difference. I get that from Exodus 33 and 3

ne I see God expressing his grace. I get that every time I see John
d what we're going to do for the rest of the week is track the Jesus
cture, that grace expressed through the book of John, as he extends
to other people.

Grace is giving people space. It has a wonderful measure of bibli-
tolerance. How many of you have ever said to somebody 'Would
i give me space?' Isn't it interesting, that we say that to others and
are very slow to give it to anyone else? We want space but nobody
gets the privilege. Grace is the benefit of the doubt. Grace is for-
ness, regardless of how deep the offence is. Grace is a heart of
ipassion that can be touched by another person's needs. Our prob-
is we always see the faults. You see someone in the ditch of life
you go 'If you hadn't done that back there, you wouldn't be down
; so you made your ditch, you can lie in it.' You know what
st consistently did because he was a God of grace? He saw
nd the faults, to see the need. Beyond every fault, under every
is a penetrating need and grace sees the need and goes after it,
lless. Let's go to the negative side, because sometimes you can
something by what it's not as well as what it is. Grace does not
the finger. God's finger is pointed right at me, that's the finger I
to worry about. Grace does not want to keep everything even,
does not keep score, and grace is not fair. How many of you are
delighted that God has not been fair with you? Are there a few
who would like God to be fair?

ce doesn't keep track, grace forgives and you think that I'm
o say grace forgives and forgets. I want to relieve you of some-
only God can forget sins. The Bible says he separates them as
he east is from the west. You and I do not have the ability to
Grace forgives but you can attach new meanings to the mem-
iat's what you can do. All those memories back there, that
was the tool of God in my life to transform me.

e attaches new memories to the past. Grace liberates, grace
instuck from living in the world of past offences. With this I
close because I want you to take this thought with you. The
of American Christianity, UK Christianity I have to assume,
Christianity is that we all know about the grace of

Christianity to us, don't we? Do you revel in the grace of God for you? Do you love to sing *Amazing Grace*? Why is it that we do not extend that grace to others? Why is it that we are so stingy with the grace that has been so full to us? There is no way you can be like Christ if you don't let that amazing grace flow out of your life to touch people around you. He touched people with his grace; he forgave the prostitute, he gave life afresh, he promised eternal life, he forgave the past. He got people unstuck; he touched this world with grace, the grace of God, and none if us could ever be satisfied with the grace of God unless we have heard the call of him to extend the grace to others.

You can't be like Jesus if you don't share his grace with the world. If you don't hear anything else, you must hear that and if you think that's a non-issue, then I want to read to you a story that Christ told. Peter had asked the profound question. 'I think I'm getting a grip on this grace thing but how many times do I have to forgive someone?' You really don't have a grip on grace if you're asking how many times you have to forgive someone. Jesus gave that classic answer, 'Seventy times seven' – which is unlimited, because that's for the same offence, not for all the offences. Then Jesus told a story, like he always did.

For this reason, the kingdom of heaven can be compared to a certain king who wished to settle his accounts with his slaves. When he had begun to settle, there was brought to him someone who owed to him ten thousand talents. But since he did not have the means to repay, his lord commanded him to be sold, along with his wife and children and all that he had, so that the payment could be made. The slave fell down and prostrated himself, saying 'Lord, have patience with me and I will repay you everything.' The lord of that slave felt compassion and released him and forgave him the debt. But that slave went out and found one of his fellow slaves who owed him a hundred denarii and he seized him and began to strangle him, saying 'Pay back what you owe!' So his fellow slave fell down and began to entreat him, saying 'Have patience with me! I promise I will repay you.' He was unwilling, however, and threw him in prison until he could pay back what he owed. So when his fellow slaves saw what had happened, they were deeply grieved and came and reported to their lord all that had happened. Then, summoning him, his lord said 'You wicked slave! I forgave you all that debt because you entreated me to. Should you not so have mercy on your fellow slave, then, as I had mercy on you?' His lord was moved with anger and handed him over to the torturers until he should pay all that was owed him. So shall my Heavenly Father do to you if each of you should not forgive his brother or extend grace from your heart.

Chapter 2
Grace applied

Introduction

Let's open God's Bible together to our text: John 1:14-18. We're going to spend all morning on one phrase, because it is so critical, in terms of us learning to ignite grace expressed through our lives. 'From his fullness have we all received'... here's the phrase we're going to talk about today...'grace upon grace. For the law was given through Moses; grace and truth came through Jesus Christ. No one has seen God: the only Son, who is in the bosom of the Father, he has made him known.'

Reliable grace

I count it interesting that Jesus left one astonishing impression on his disciples. Our theme this week is to be followers of Christ. To be examples, we need to know the lead issue of Jesus' life was that he was a person of reliable grace. Or, if we go all the way to the cross, we might say that he was a God of extreme grace, grace that extended to an instrument of cruel torture, where he would prove the maximum of grace to die for sinners like you and me.

I find myself wondering what they'll think of me after I'm gone. I'm so impressed that John had one memory of Jesus, that he was a person of reliable grace. Wouldn't it be the height of legacy, if they would say of you, 'You know the thing I remember most? Every time I intersected their life I was touched by such reliable grace.' If they say that about you, that would mean that you had become like Christ. What will they say about you, when you're gone? Will it match what they said about Jesus?

Getting to the summit of living that kind of a life is a phenomenal challenge for us. We are not naturally inclined toward qualities of grace. Grace is about giving, grace is about helping. We are bent far more towards personal gains, living for our own interests, feelings, desires, rights and privileges. The generosities of grace come very hard when life is all about me. Life being all about me gets so in the way of a grace-filled life. Maybe you go to church and you say, 'I didn't get anything at all out of the message.' Get a biblical life; it's not always all about you. Grace cares about whether God had the message for some-body else. Was Jesus preached? Was the truth proclaimed? But it's always so much about me and it'll always be getting in the way of grace. 'I don't like the music.' 'Kids are ruining the church.' I'm fifty nine so I've finally woken up to something. I've had my day in church, I've had my hymns, I've had my songs, I've had my way of doing church and I'm on my way out. I'm rooting for the kids. They are the church that is coming. I work with fifteen hundred of the finest kids on this globe at Moody and they have such passion for Christ. And you say, 'I know but he wears his cap to church.' The issue is not his cap, the issue is the heart that beats under that cap and I just want you to know some of those hearts beat with a deeper, richer passion for Christ than ours. This challenge of a grace-extending life: the prob-lem of me always gets in the way.

Isn't that the very essence of the fall? In the beginning God created this perfect environment and brought Eve to be with Adam. Eve was created to be a help mate, to surrender to her God and to be a gov-erness of the garden. It was all about those kinds of things until the tempter arrived and it would no longer be about being a help mate and a surrendered woman to God and a governess of the garden: it would all now be about Eve. Satan said, 'This could make you wise.' It is the essence of the fall and until we get a grip on that and get victory by God's grace we will never live a life that extends the grace of Christ to anybody else.

Grace focuses on people

Not only does grace get blocked by the problem of ourselves, the second issue of the blockage of grace through us is that grace is tough because its focus is on people. I've always thought that ministry would be a cake walk if it weren't for people. We're far better at holding grudges and plotting revenge than giving space and forgiving those who offend us. Our minds are prone to rush to judgement, before considering giving the gift of understanding. Our bent towards 'not grace' living encourages us in this unhealthy preoccupation with ourselves that devastates relationships. Grace is meant to make relationships, but because we are not inclined towards grace, we tend to divide and decimate and destroy relationships. And, in that way, we destroy the glory of God.

But, more serious than any of that, the downsides of living on the collision course of a graceless life is the reality that a life that is void of grace denies the very heart of the mission of Jesus. He came to grace our graceless world with the divine gift of his abundant kindness. That's the mark of his mission; he did it to the extreme and no one who crossed his path was exempt from the benefit of the touch of his grace. And this was not just so that he could be what we would expect a good person to be. His reliable grace was the authentic imprint of his claim to be God, because that's what God was. For us to ignore the importance of grace, as a leading quality in our lives, is to deny our calling to reflect the character and quality of Jesus. A life that has a spotty track record of grace is a life that fails to bring glory to God. It is no small thing to ignore the issue of grace through your life.

I find myself wondering why is it that a church born by grace, blessed by grace, sustained by grace, strengthened by grace, supported by grace, whose hymnals are full of songs about grace, how is it that a church like that can appear to be so very graceless? How could it be; being born by grace, blessed by grace, supported and sustained by grace, how could we be so very graceless? It does not make sense. Philip Yancey, in his book *What's so amazing about grace?* tells the story of a friend of his who works with down-and-out people in Chicago.

> A prostitute came to me in wretched straits, homeless, sick, unable to buy food for her two-year-old daughter. Through sobs and tears, she told me that she had been renting out her daughter – two years old! – to men interested in kinky sex. She made more money renting out her daughter for an hour than she could earn on her own in a night. She had to do it, she said, to support her own drug habit. I could hardly bear hearing her sordid story. For one thing, it made me legally liable – I'm required to report cases of child abuse. I had no idea what to say to this woman.
>
> At last I asked if she'd ever thought of going to a church for help. I will never forget the look of pure, naive shock that crossed her face. "Church!" she cried. "Why would I ever go there? I was already feeling terrible about myself. They'd just make me feel worse."[1]

Yancey concludes with this profound and penetrating statement. 'What struck me about my friend's story is that women like this prostitute fled toward Jesus, not away from him. The worse a person felt about herself, the more likely she saw Jesus as a refuge. Has the church lost that gift? Evidently the down-and-out, who flocked to Jesus when he lived on earth, no longer feel welcome among his followers. What has happened?'[2]

Transition to a grace-filled life

I would like to have all of us who are taking this seriously become a little more remedial and see if the text of God's word can't help us

---

[1] Philip Yancey, *What's so amazing about grace?* (London: Harper Collins 1997) p11

[2] Yancey, p11

with the transition. Let me mark the transition from a self-absorbed, usually graceless life, to a life that is full of the grace of Jesus Christ, extended to others. I want us to go to this phrase in verse 16, 'For, of his fullness, we have all received'. Then John explains this fullness that they have received, that it is grace upon grace.

Now, unfortunately, many of us tend to be entangled in the attitudes of the system of the law. That is the road block that John tackles in this verse. The first thing we must ask is 'What does he mean, grace upon grace?' Literally in the Greek, this is 'grace for grace' or 'grace upon grace'. Any time you have a question like that, the first thing you do is flee to the context. Verse 17 begins with this word 'for'. 'For' is an explanatory word. John's saying 'For the law was given through Moses but reliable grace was realised through Jesus Christ.' This says 'grace upon grace' and the next verse is an explanatory verse. He mentions two commodities and what are they? What did Moses give us? The law. What did Jesus bring? Grace. I need to talk a little bit about the law and grace.

Grace and law

There are four things that will help unwrap this for us. You and I need to know that the law, that God gave in the Old Testament, was a gift of God's grace. I believe what he is speaking about here, the first grace, is the grace of the law. That's a little shocking for most of us who have seen the Bible as 'the Old Testament's law, the New Testament's grace.' Let me tell you about the grace of the law. God gave the law to resolve moral chaos. Before the law came, everybody could do whatever they wanted, there were no moral standards, no organisational elements. There was nothing to stem the chaos and the anarchy of people living all on their own. So God intersected our planet in that wonderful, revelatory moment with the law, to give us order in the midst of moral chaos, to give us that which is right and good.

We should never despise the law: it was a gift of God's grace. Think of a planet without a moral code. Think of the western world, Britain and America. Can you already began to feel the moral anarchy that is seeping back in, as the grace of the law begins to depart from our western culture? I love Psalm 1:1, 'Happy is the man who does not live in his own ways of moral chaos but who delights in the law of the Lord and meditates in it day and night.' It orders your life and brings you peace and joy and happiness.

In Romans chapter 8, Paul writes 'the law is holy and righteous and good.' Let me ask you another question. How would you even know that you needed a Saviour, if it weren't for the law? That's why our world despises the righteous standards of God because if you have that, then you know you have to meet the standard. If you take that away, then you take the need for a Saviour away. We need to know, number one, that the law is a gift of God's grace; secondly, the law did have some shortcomings. Not that God made some mistakes in it but it was not complete. If the law was complete, we would not have needed Jesus to come and fulfil the law. The law had some inherent inadequacies and most of them were the kind of attitudes that they spawned. I want to camp on the attitude thing because I think it helps us in this transition to a grace-filled life.

First of all, the law emphasised consequences and not resolution. The law emphasised things like fairness, keeping everything even. The law emphasised an eye for an eye and a tooth for a tooth. So the law tended to foster attitudes that lived in consequences; everything needing to be even and fair in life. It was those attitudes that Jesus came to fight against because those are the very attitudes, in our own lives, that keep us from living grace-filled lives. Jesus talks about grace being layered with another grace because grace does not obliterate the law. For any of us who may be stuck in this mind-set that grace is now here and the law is now gone, nothing could be further from the truth. This is grace, 'grace layering itself on top of grace' taking us to the next step of grace. We live in a world that wants to believe that everything should be loving, merciful, kind, gracious and good and therefore we don't need the law. A grace without the standards is a devastating commodity. I've been following whether or not actively gay priests should be ordained and most recently, should be made bishops. The other night, I was watching a round table discussion with a lady and an Anglican rector, who were on the side of the authority of Scripture. That's really the issue. The homosexuality is quite secondary to the authority of Scripture. Will Scripture rule the church?

There was another couple who were advocating the openness of the gay lifestyle for priests and bishops and about seven or eight minutes into the discussion, the gay priest says, 'I haven't heard anything, at all, about Jesus and about his love. I want you to know that I am committed to a long-term, loving relationship with my partner and we love each other and we are faithful to each other. That is what Jesus celebrated.' What he was really saying there is that grace obliterates the law. Since we have this grace, this loving, committed relationship to each other, which Jesus celebrates, the law is a non-issue.

I want you to know that the law is never a non-issue. The law is the righteous standards of a righteous God. God didn't give us the law to make it hard on ourselves. God gave us the law to reveal what his true righteousness was like. The law's a direct connect to the image of God. God is always truth; therefore he never lies: therefore the standard of a true God is that we don't lie to one another. God is always faithful to what is righteous, therefore he doesn't cheat. God is faithful to his vows, therefore he would never be unfaithful to a marriage partner. All of the law is a direct reflection of the very nature of God. Jesus can't obliterate the law, it's totally impossible. But, if you buy the line that the gay priest was trying to build his case on, it takes us back to moral chaos.

Let's say that we believe the only standard that really is valid is our love for each other in long-term, committed relationships. If that is our standard by which we judge moral activity, then wouldn't it be OK for a thirty year old guy to come and say, 'I have this eleven-year-old boy in my neighbourhood and we love each other and we are committed to a long-term relationship.' I think the principle is the same. When you obliterate the law, you just open the door to return to moral chaos. That's why it's important for us to see this connection of grace upon grace. The law was grace and Jesus came to complete the inadequacies of grace.

Grace brings resolution

God's grace resolves the inadequacies of the law. Jesus spent so much of his time working on these attitudes that were residual, the inadequacies of the law that life is all about consequences: you do that and you die. Read the Gospels, see Jesus working hard to bring this new grace system into place; it is so vitally important. I would like us to track the teachings of Jesus at some very crucial moments.

Jesus and the Pharisees

Luke chapter 15; Jesus is at the core of the crowd with interested people but we learn that these people are tax collectors and sinners. The Pharisees had this 'good guys, bad guys' theology, which is not hard to get if all you have is the grace of the law. We are the good guys and God loves us because we are the good people in this world. But there's a lot of bad guys in this world and they will be subject to God's judgement. That was their theology: no room for grace or mercy. You constantly watch this in the gospels, where the Pharisees and the scribes are marginalising the subculture of people like tax collectors, sinners, prostitutes, all the really bad people.

Jesus was at the core of the crowd with tax collectors and sinners and around the fringe of the crowd were the scribes and the Pharisees and they were murmuring 'He is with the tax collectors and sinners.' They had that on Jesus because – back to their good guys, bad guys theology – Jesus came and claimed to be God. So if you were in this law/consequence mind-set, if somebody hit this planet and said, 'I'm God in the flesh,' who do you think he ought to hang out with? The good guys. It did not add up, that Jesus came and claimed to be God and he's spending time with those kind of people. And when you're really ticked at someone, you bring up all the bad stuff and throw it at them at the same time. They say 'He eats with them too.' In that day if you ate with somebody, their dinners were long and it was a sign of fellowship, of receiving someone.

Jesus was willing to invade the bad parts of his world, in the face of consequences, with the grace of resolution. That's the juxtaposition: the law tended to do consequences, grace moves us to resolution, forgiveness, restoration, not to consequences. So Jesus, to try to straighten out their theology, in Luke chapter 15 tells three stories: the story of the sheep, the story of the lost coin and the story of the lost son. The first two stories made the point that if you'd lost something of value, you'd go after it. All the bad people in your town have value to God. He created them, sin has robbed them, he has suffered a significant loss and he would like to go after them, through you.

The prodigal son

I want to talk to you about the story of the prodigal son. Prodigal stories were rampant in the land, they had lots of prodigal stories. They all ran about the same as Jesus' story. There was this younger child and then he decided to take off and he took all and went to a foreign land, did a whole bunch of naughty things. And when he got home, he was in big trouble. The moral of the story being, 'Don't you ever do what he did, because if you ever try to come home, you're going to get nailed.' Just put that as the backdrop to Jesus telling this story.

One thing you also need to know in this story is the offence that the prodigal commits against the father is not the naughty things he did in the foreign land. This boy asked for his inheritance. If you ask for the inheritance ahead of time, you are saying, in that eastern culture, 'I wish you were dead.' You couldn't have a deeper offence against your father. In those days they didn't have pensions. The pensions were the property, and younger sons managed the land and kept income coming from the land so you, as an older person, could have the income. The land and the stock and everything were the pensions. He sold the land, offended the dignity of the family, cashed out the retirement fund and wasted it so he could never repay it. Here is the point of the story that Jesus is making: sin is not just this horizontal problem, it is a direct offence against the almighty God.

The issue of sin is you have offended the almighty God who sees all things, that's what Jesus was saying. Jesus could not have painted a bigger picture of offence and sin in their minds and they're going, 'This kid's going to get it when he gets home.' Then he says that the father waited, every day, to see his son coming back. Now, if you were a Pharisee and you were living in a world of the grace of the law, which tended to make you be more into consequences, he was waiting there with some big stick in his hand.

'When the father saw the son from a long way off, his heart was struck with compassion.' This was a shock to these law people because their brains were so different. And so, he runs and embraces this smelly, wasted child and kisses him, which is a sign of full family acceptance. They head towards home and he yells ahead 'Kill the fatted calf, we're going to have a party, bring the best robe, bring shoes,' which was a sign that he was no longer a slave. And the ring, the sign of authority of the family; this was full, unconditional restoration. Do you see the transition? He's working hard to get people into this new era, to this grace upon grace reality.

Then we hear about the elder brother, who's coming in from the fields. It's such a big party, he hears the songs and the dancing from afar and he says to a servant, 'I didn't know there was a party, what's going on?' He said, 'Your brother's home!' 'That guy!' and he says to his father 'He has wasted all of our resources and you have thrown a party for him. But I have been faithful to you. I never left. I put in a hard day's work for you and you have never thrown a party for me.'

How many of you think he's got a point? Is there anybody here who is thankful that God has not been fair with you? If he had been fair with me, there would have been the consequence of judgement on my life. But he came to bring grace upon grace, that there might be restoration, reconciliation and celebration that a sinner has come home. And the fact that you and I think the guy's got a point tells us how lost we are back in that old system. It ought to be a very convicting thing that we're more about what's fair than about what grace is all about. It's that transition that Jesus is trying to make.

Jesus tells another really wonderful story in Matthew chapter 20.

The labourers in the vineyard

This is a grace upon grace story, this is the story about the labourers in the vineyard. Just remember what Jesus is trying to do: he's trying to get us over into the new system, he's trying to get us up a notch into the grace upon grace perspective.

This guy's got a harvest and all of a sudden he needs some more workers. He goes into the village, early in the morning and he tries to rally these people to come and he says, 'I'll pay you a denarius for a day's work.' So they go and they start, the sun comes up and they're working like crazy, they can't wait for the pay line at the end of the day. Half way through the day, the manager suddenly realises that he doesn't have enough labour, so he goes and gets some more. And, about an hour before it's up, he goes and gets some more.

So the day's over and they're all standing in the pay line. And when the hour guys get up there, they get full pay!

'You what?'!

How many of you think those guys have a point? You're still back in this whole thought of consequence and everything's got to be fair and even and you have no clue about what Jesus brought to this planet; resolution and restoration and being generous, for a change. What really strikes me is what Jesus says that the lord said to these gripping, complaining people. Verse 13; he said to one of them: 'Friend, I am doing you no wrong. Didn't you agree with me for a denarius? We signed the contract, what's the deal?'

'The deal is what you did for those other guys!'

So he says, 'Take what is yours and go your way but I wish to give to this last man the same as you. Is it not lawful for me to do what I wish with what is my own?'

We're going to learn tomorrow that one of the marks of grace is phenomenal generosity. But if you're locked into this system of law/consequence, which is one of the inadequacies of the law, it tends to breed that attitude. You'll always be cutting for what's yours and watching everybody else. My wife's pastor used to speak of the New Testament passage that says 'Rejoice with them that rejoice and weep with them that weep.' He said, 'It's a lot easier to weep with them that weep than it is to rejoice with them that rejoice.' If you start feeling envious in your heart about someone who's got something more than you've gotten, it is a signal you are stuck in the oldness of the law and have not made the transition yet to the grace of Jesus Christ.

Take the Sermon on the Mount. It was a very shocking thing for these guys to hear the words of the Sermon on the Mount. 'If somebody comes and slaps you in the face, turn the other cheek.' In the law, if somebody came and slapped you in the face, 'We have to keep this even.' Slap, slap. And the guy you slap back says, 'I've got to keep this even.' So it's bam bam bam. Do you know what Jesus is saying? His grace is so liberating. If someone comes and slaps you in the face, grace says, 'Slap me on the other cheek, because I'm not going to get stuck here with you.' The thing about the law, with everything needing to be fair: you get stuck there. You get bogged down in the mire of keeping score. And Jesus says, 'I have come to bring grace to liberate you; don't do this slap for slap thing.' I love that about grace. Someone comes and says, 'Give me your coat.' 'Sure, I've got another one in the closet, you want that one too?' Someone says, 'I'm taking you to court.' Say, 'Forget it, let's settle. I'm not going to do this with you.' It's wonderful, isn't it? This wonderful liberation of the grace that Jesus kept teaching, to try to transition us into this grace that he brought for us.

You say 'What happens if we have a legitimate offence?' In Matthew chapter 18, Jesus made very clear there's a process you can follow. Number one: you go to the person alone, so we're not talking to all of our friends about this. If they don't hear, we take back a trusted friend. And if they don't hear us we take the matter to the church and if they don't hear the church, it says, 'At that point you shake the dust off your feet.'

You've done everything you can do; sure it's not fair. Don't get stuck! Go on, live in grace, let God take care of your offender. Isn't this wonderful? I find this whole grace upon grace thing to be such a liberating thing in my heart and in my soul. And the issue that remains for us is: where are you? Though you have said you are a New Testament believer, in the age of grace, isn't it interesting how much of us are still firmly planted in the attitudes of the law? Jesus came and said, 'I have something better for you, follow me and put grace upon grace.'

Chapter 3
Aspects of grace

Introduction

Guess where we're going in God's word? John chapter 1 verse 14. We are in the prologue of the book of John, verses 1 through 18, where John sets up the rest of the book. Locked into the prologue are hints as to the themes of the book and there's several different tracking themes through John. Probably the major one is that Jesus makes a claim and backs up that claim with a sign that illustrates and authenticates the claim he was making about himself.

We would expect that if John sets up that his deepest impression about Christ was that Christ reflected what he knew God to be, then that might be a hint as to what is to come. As you read the Gospel of John, with that thought in mind, you begin seeing all these grace encounters open up. In fact it becomes definitive of different ways in which we can express grace, as we are seeking to become like Jesus.

Let me read through these verses again, then we're going to go back to verse 14 to isolate eight marks of a grace-extending life. 'And the Word became flesh and dwelt amongst us and we beheld his glory. It was the glory of the only begotten from the Father. John bore witness to him and cried out, saying, "This was he of whom I said, 'He who comes after me has higher rank than I, for he existed before me.' " '

John, when he inserts the testimony of John the Baptist, is again verifying the authenticity of Jesus' messiahship. He's working overtime to underscore the authenticity of the person of Christ and his claim to be God. After he does that, he picks up the theme again. 'For of his fullness we have all received grace upon grace. For the law was given through Moses, grace and truth were realised through Jesus Christ. No one has seen God at any time; the only begotten Son, who is in the bosom of the Father, he has explained him.'

What does God require of you?

We're going to do eight marks of a grace-extending life, but before we do that, I'm going to add a biblical backdrop to this whole theme. My dad, every time he signed a letter, always put under his name 'Isaiah 58: 10 and 11.' It was his life verse. I call Isaiah 58 a whining passage. Israel is getting in the face of God and whinging 'Lord, what on earth does it take to release your power?' Then they go through this long litany, 'We fast, we keep all the feasts, we have our daily devotions. We do all these things we think are expected of us but yet you seem so far away.' That's for all of us here who keep all the rules and wonder why we feel such a distance. It could be because you're living in Isaiah 58. Listen to what God says in response:

> Is not this the fast which I have chosen;
> to loosen the bonds of wickedness,
> to undo the bands of the yoke,
> to let the oppressed go free and to break every yoke?
> Is it not for you to divide your bread with the hungry,
> and to bring the homeless poor into the house;
> when you see the naked, to cover him
> and not to hide yourself from your own flesh?

And after you do that,

> The Lord will continually guide you,
> and satisfy your desire with good things,
> and give you strength in your bones.
> You will be like a watered garden,
> and like a spring of water whose waters do not fail.

You know what God's saying? You don't live to touch your world with my grace. What a convicting thought that we could be involved in all the right things, yet God would not be pleased with us because we are not people of extending grace. God takes it very seriously. God's with those who have needs.

Justice and mercy

There's another, Micah 6:8. Israel, again, is whinging: 'What does it take to please you?' God comes back and gives them a short list. He says, 'Have I not told you what is good and what is required of you? That you love mercy, that you are passionately addicted to the exercise of mercy.' You say, 'That's not grace.' It is. The words mercy and grace and love, in both the Old and the New Testaments, all merge. They have their own distinct nuances but there are many passages where they are used interchangeably. Mercy is giving to people, relieving their guilt, forgiving them, when they don't deserve it. It's grace in action.

Number two: to do justice doesn't mean that you go around judging people. It means that you live a just life. Grace means that you are fair in all of your dealings, with everybody. The issue is, when people, when life is not fair to you, that's when the grace of Jesus Christ kicks in. What does it take to please God? To be passionately addicted to mercy, grace and to be a person who lives justly and walks humbly with your God. That's on the short list on how to please God. Can I give you just one more? Colossians chapter 3, talking about the transforming power of our redemption, verse 12 says, 'And so, as those who have been chosen of God, holy and beloved.' Then he says, 'Here is what the chosen of God, holy and beloved ought to look like.' And he

starts this rather long list of qualities. What really surprises me is that
the very first thing on the list is compassion. God is looking for compassion in your life. And if you don't think that compassion is a part
of grace, then you missed the first day when we made that very clear,
when God prefaces the *hesed/emit* formula that John repeats by saying
to Moses 'You want to know my ways? I'm a God of compassion; slow
to anger, willing to forgive.'

A grace extending life

Now, let's go back to John 1:14; eight marks of a grace-extending life
and we're going to take the segments of this verse because it is literally profound in its meaning. We're going to start with what he meant
by 'the Word'. It is the Greek word *logos* and the Greek philosophers,
who would think about the meaning of life and try to solve all the
riddles of life, kept thinking, 'Somewhere in the universe, there has to
be something, where all of these insoluble questions and issues are
resolved.' They gave that unknown god, that place, a word, *logos*. John
says, 'You're looking for the logos? You're looking for the answers to
the questions of your life? You find that in Jesus Christ.'

Mark 1: Solution

Jesus Christ, the fullest expression of grace, is, by his very nature, the
ultimate solution. When I think about grace, grace is always resolution. In life, are you a part of the problem or part of the solution?
When you walk into a room, filled with conflict, do people know this
is going to be someone who will contribute toward resolution? That's
a mark of the grace-extending believer, that like Jesus, we become a
part of a solution. The ultimate proof of that is the cross where he
solved the worst unanswerable problem of life, the hopelessness and
the decadence and the despair of sin.

Mark 2: Transition

'And the Word became'. . . Let's stop there. What does that mean? It's
a hint to the beginning of the incarnation, the almighty Creator

coming and living on our planet. At one point in eternity past there was an eternal decree that Jesus would come as the solution to our deepest problems and a part of that eternal decree meant that he had to leave the comforts of heaven. He leaves all of that applause to transition, to become, to come here with us. Now you say, 'How does that apply to a grace-filled life?'

Jesus came here on a mission of grace. You and I are called to a mission of grace. It's what it means to be like Jesus Christ. There has to be a measure of transition, of becoming, of moving toward that goal. It is going to mean, for a lot of us, that we leave the comforts of our lives and start to become a mission of grace to some segment of our world. It's not going to be real comfortable: grace is not a comfortable business. Jesus was not called to comfort, he left his comfort to get grace done. The real issue of whether or not you are a grace-extender is whether or not you are farther along becoming more a grace-extender today than you were last year. It's not talking about perfection, it's talking about progress.

Mark 3: Identity

'The Word,' solution 'became,' transition 'flesh,' identity. Philippians 2 tells us that we ought to have the mind of Christ and if you say 'What did that mean?' it means that he gave up all the glory of heaven and poured himself out to us. He came to this planet and was found in the likeness of people like you and me. Is it an amazing thing to you that when the King of the universe came, he came and chose to be found in our flesh, to be like you and me? He did it so that he could identify with us, so that the writer to Hebrews could give this assurance to us that, 'We have a high priest who is not untouched by the feelings of our infirmities. But because we have this high priest we can come with unstaggering confidence before the throne, that we might find grace and mercy in our time of need (Heb. 4:15,16).

Of course, there is a soteriological issue there; he had to be there to save us but even that is identifying with our sin. He took all our sin on him at the grace moment of the cross. It's identity and how important, if I am to be an extender of grace, that I must become incarnated in other people lives, and stop standing off as a fault finder, but rather get past that stuff to the real needs.

Mark 4: Relationships

'And the Word became flesh and dwelt among us'... It literally means that Jesus came and pitched his tent in our midst, he was going to live in our neighbourhood. This is about relating, about being willing to engage. He came to relate to us personally. Read through the Gospels and look at all the kinds of people that he related to. This is the scary part about extending grace. It calls for us to begin to move into relationships in which you can pour the grace of God. Please bust out of your holy huddle, the 'us three and no more' mentality. You say 'I know a few people, I could do a mission of grace in their lives but it is really risky. I don't know if I want to bear that risk. I might get rejected.'

For all of you who have that kind of stuff in your heart right now, I want to ask you a question. Was it a major, ultimate, eternal risk for Jesus to pitch his tent among us? Yes. The grace of Jesus gave him the courage and resolve to come here and be among us even at great risk to himself. When you start embarking on this grace venture, you're going to need a big dose of real trust in God because it is going to be scary a lot of the time. You are going to feel vulnerable, but I want you to know the least risky place to be is where Jesus is. Jesus is bound and determined to be involved in relationships where grace can flow and he is looking for something that's got skin on it to be a middle person in a grace transaction between you and somebody who desperately needs you. Regardless of the risk, follow him, he'll take care of you.

Mark 5: Observation

'The Word became flesh and we beheld. . .' A life marked by extended grace: your grace will be observable, people will see your grace. It's not that Jesus wrote these nice letters from on top of some mountain about grace: the grace flowing out of his life was, literally, an observable reality. I think that we increasingly live in a world where people do not want to hear what we have to say. How do you reach a world that doesn't want to hear what you have to say? Jesus solved the dilemma, in Matthew chapter 5:14-16, where he said this, 'You are the light of the world,' and then he summarises that in verse 16 and tells us what it means to be the light of the world.

When they stop listening to us they're still watching us, in fact they're probably watching us more than they have ever watched us before. Here is the formula that Jesus gave to the New Testament church. 'Let your light so shine that people may see . . .' There was something observable about Jesus that struck a chord in the needy world. 'That they may see your good works,' that's the definition of the light. What is the light? It is the good works flowing out of your life. There's two words that are used in the New Testament for good, connected with works. And one of them is *agathos*, which means to be good righteously, to keep the rules, to be straight. The other is *kalos*. What Jesus uses is the word *kalos*, here. Because, generally speaking, your righteous behaviour does not seem compelling, to someone on the outside.

For instance, you go up to some person at work, who doesn't know Christ, and say, 'You ought to come to Jesus because then you could tithe.' That doesn't have a whole lot of power to it! Or you say, 'You need to come to Jesus because then you could go to church every Sunday.' They say, 'I don't want to go to church every Sunday. I work five days a week, I like my weekend!' Or 'You ought to come to Jesus and you wouldn't have to sleep around any more.' They want to sleep around!

I'm not saying that righteousness isn't important, *agathos* is critically important. Don't bale out on *agathos* but don't count on *agathos* to be the light that becomes a compelling, credible impact in your world. *Kalos* are good works that are beautiful, amazing, unique, that catch people's attention, consistently in the New Testament. *Kalos* works are the kind of works that are works of love extended; touching people with love, doing something for the downtrodden, helping somebody who is in need. It is the active works of my life that demonstrate clearly the wonderful grace of God extended to me and now extended to other people.

The early church lived and moved in a world much like our world, a pagan world with open spirituality and a multiplicity of gods and no moral authority and no accountability. A world that despised the claim that Jesus was the only way, the only truth and the only life. It was their observable works of grace to their world, that their world could not deny. For instance, in those days, if you had a baby girl or a child who was born with a handicap, they had a practice that was called death by exposure. They took that baby and put it out, often on the dung heaps outside the city gate, and let it die. Do you know what Christians did? You read the secular literature, about the early church, they note these kind of things all the time. They went out and harvested these little babies, brought them into their homes, cleaned them up and reared them. Don't you think, that observable work of grace caught the attention of a watching world?

Saint Laurence, the church treasurer in a region, was asked by the Roman authorities to bring the treasures of the church to the Roman government. He said, 'It'll take me a little bit of time to get that done.' They said, 'You have eight days.' Eight days later he brought widows, orphans, the lame, blind and impoverished people and said, 'These are the treasures of the church.' That's how seriously they took this observable behaviour of grace, and a watching world couldn't ignore that. They used to go on seasons of fasts. You and I fast because we want a real special answer to prayer. They fasted so that, after the season of fasting, they could collect the money they would have spent, to give the money to the poor. And, in that day, the poor had a real need. They loved the poor and it caught the attention of their world.

One more illustration of this observablity of grace and the power of it. There were two major plagues that struck the Roman empire. In the second plague in the second century, one out of every five Roman citizens died. As soon as the plague hit a town, people fled to the mountains for the clean air. People left their children, left their family members. It was the Christians, who stayed in town, and many of them died, who took these people, nursed them back to health, when it was possible. Don't you think, that if you had been left by your family, nursed back to health by these weird, despicable Christians, that, maybe, that observable act of grace might have a little bit of power?

So, when we read that Jesus, the solution, in transition, identified himself and dropped himself right into his relationships, so that we could behold something about him, I have to ask you this question. What does your world see in your life? Just a touch of the observability of the glory of God and his grace, extended through you? And I have to ask myself that question.

Mark 6: The divine signature

'We beheld his glory, the glory as of the only begotten of the Father.' This was the mark of his divinity. It was this grace and truth, this reliable grace, that was the signature of God on his life. It was what marked him, they saw the glory of God. It was what affirmed his claim to be divine. 'Stowell, have good luck, trying to apply that to us. We're not divine so we can skip this mark of a grace-extended life.' I would if Jesus hadn't had given a last command; John 13: 34 and 35, 'A new command I give you that you love . . .'

We're going to stop right there because what's the difference between love and grace? There is very little difference, in fact the Old Testament word *hesed*, that we learned about on Monday, God's loyal covenant love, the Hebrew word is translated in the New Testament *charis*, his grace. Now, *agape* love in the New Testament is seeing a need and giving to that need, regardless, because I do it as an act of my will, not as a response and not as an emotional thing. And suddenly you begin to see that the definitions of these words tend to merge. Now, there are some unique nuances between love and grace that make them a little different but they merge. Was it the grace of Jesus that led him to love you at the cross, or was it his love that triggered the grace of him towards you at the cross?

I'm struck by the fact that Jesus said, 'By this shall all men know.' In America we have this little phrase that 'really good Christians don't drink, dance, smoke, chew, go with girls that do'. And the rules are very important, if they're biblical rules. Jesus said 'By this shall all men know that you are my disciples if you show grace, one to another, if you love one another.' It is especially towards the household of faith. They're watching how we treat each other. It is the divine signature on your life, that you live in grace with your brother and sister in Christ. 'All men know that you are my followers' (conditional clause) 'if you are a person of extending love to your brothers and sisters in Christ.' A mark of the divine.

Mark 7: Fullness

'The Word became flesh and dwelt among us and we beheld his glory,' the divine signature, 'as of the only begotten Son, full of grace and truth.' Literally, the Greek word means the fullness of grace and truth. You know the lake that's at Keswick; you could take a cup of water of the lake water and you could say, 'This is the lake water', would that be right? But is it the fullness of the lake water? No. The fullness of the lake is all of the water in the lake. It's not that Jesus just happened to be full of a little bit of the grace of God: in his life, he was the manifest fullness of it. He was the totality, the maximum, the extreme of it, there was no discounting or compromise, he was totally, fully all that the grace of God was and is and ever more will be. And the mark of a true grace extender, who is climbing to that peak, to become like Christ and have this mark on their life is that your grace is not an on and off thing. It is limitless, it is the fullness of grace, it applies to all kinds of people and all kinds of situations because Jesus was the fullness.

Mark 8: Experience

The last mark of a grace-extending life is that grace is to be, not just observable but experienced. He says of Jesus and of this grace, 'have we all received.' John experienced the grace of God, Christ in his life. The question then, for us, must be who around your life, today, would come up to me, afterwards, and say, 'Joe, I just want to tell you I've been hanging out with Barbara, I've been hanging out with Nigel and Cameron and I want you know I have been touched by their grace. The grace of Jesus has touched me through their lives.' Is there anybody, around you, who say, 'I have experienced that'? Can you name them? Can you name the moment? Could it be that, maybe, somebody could say that about you because today you started up to that peak of being like Christ? And these eight marks would mark your life with the reality of Jesus, in you and through you.

I've had a lot, particularly when I was in the pastoral ministry, of very difficult situations in terms of people's tragedies but I don't think that I ever had one quite this difficult. There's a lady in our church and her husband was a mission executive. His name was Phil Armstrong. He'd be gone a lot and his wife had kept the home. He was retiring and they'd bought a little piece of property in the mountains, in North Carolina. Finally she was getting Phil back, and she'd given him to the Lord, her whole life, and loved the thought of them being able to spend time together. I got a call one Sunday morning, saying Phil had been up in Alaska, that weekend, in a little private missionary plane, and the plane had disappeared from the radar. They never found the plane, they never found Phil, there was no closure. I had to go to his wife's Sunday school class and call her out and share the bad news, that Phil's plane had gone down. And we stuck with Bobby, we tried to comfort her and touch her with the grace of God.

A few weeks later she came to me. I said 'How's it going, Bobby?' She said, 'It hurts so bad. I think I keep seeing him walking, when I'm in a mall. But you know what happened to me in the church foyer today? Somebody came up to me, put their arms around me and held me close and never said a word.' What she said next was so instructive, for those of us who want someone else to experience the grace of Jesus. She said, 'It was like the arms of God around my life!' Somebody in that church who brought a grace experience to someone and she was touched by God's grace. That's what it means to be a grace-extender.

Many of you are familiar with the *Jesus* film project. Paul Eshleman is the visionary founder and he told me this story. He had gone to Warner films, in Hollywood, because he wanted to do some international distribution of the films and he got a meeting at Warner films. He walks into this panelled boardroom and all these marketing guys are sitting around, who are willing to help him with some ideas. The chairman, a Jewish marketing executor, chaired the meeting.

Paul said to me, 'The meeting was very helpful but I've got to tell you what happened after the meeting. This Jewish chairman of the meeting came to me and he said, "Paul, could I talk to you?" We went in his office and he sat down and said "Paul, I need your help. Some time ago my wife and I had this baby and it became ill and the doctor told us we might lose this baby. One day I was just walking down the hall upstairs and I noticed our maid's door was ajar and she was on her knees. Later in that day, I said, 'How come you were down on your knees?' She said, 'Oh, I was praying.'

'You pray?'

'Ever since we heard about the baby, I pray every day, several times that God will heal your baby.'"

He said, to Paul, 'Thankfully, God answered her prayer. But you know where my heart really is today? My wife has been diagnosed with very serious cancer. The other day I was so distraught I went walking down the street to the synagogue and thought, maybe I could find some help. I forgot it was bingo night and kept walking and there was a church a few blocks later, the doors were wide open. I walked into the church and the minister was there. He said, "Can I help you?" and I poured my heart out to this guy and the guy prayed with me. The next day, I went to the hospital and the doctor said to me, "Aren't you Jewish?"

"Yeah, I am Jewish."

He said, "What was that minister doing here all night, last night, sitting by your wife's bed, and ministering to her?"'

Then the man paused and tears started down his cheeks and he said, 'You know? I have to tell you that last week our maid died. Paul, I have nobody to get me to God, can you help me?' Before Paul left that office, that Jewish executor was on his knees, welcoming Jesus into his life.

I want you to know what opened that door for the gospel to drive through most profoundly was people touching other people with the grace of Jesus Christ in observable, incarnational, dramatic, experiential ways. A maid, who has no power but to pray and a minister who works overtime, with no extra pay because he is committed to touching his world with the grace of Jesus Christ. And it was so observable and so experiential. Because of extended grace, that's how important this is.

Chapter 4
Becoming a grace-extender

Introduction

In the church, we literally have volumes on the grace of God and what that grace means. Unfortunately, we don't have much literature on the call in our lives, to not only know of the grace of God but to then extend that grace to others around us, so that we can be like Christ and glorify God, as he glorified God when he extended grace. It has been my passion this week that we move past being satisfied knowing about the grace of God and accept the wonderful challenge of extending that grace in our world. So what we've been doing is charting a biblical theology of grace extended or grace applied. I want us to move into application mode so that you can have some distinct things to target and a framework about how you can be an extender of grace, that you might be like Christ, that you might bring glory to God.

Let's open our Bibles to John chapter 1, beginning in verse 14. We're going to work on bringing absolute clarity to the matter of grace. Then we're going to talk about eight snapshots through the book of John, seeing how Jesus applied grace. Those will be patterns for us to apply grace, as well.

Let's read: 'And the Word became flesh and he pitched his tent among us. And we beheld his glory. He was the fullness of grace and truth. And John bore witness of him and cried out saying "This was he of whom I said 'He who comes after me has higher rank than I, for he existed before me.'" For, of his fullness, we have all received grace. For the law was given through Moses, grace and truth was realised through Jesus Christ. No man has seen God at any time; the only begotten Son, who is in the bosom of the Father, he has explained God.'

Love, grace and mercy

I want to make sure that the three Bible words that move in and out of grace are clear in our minds and they are: love, grace and mercy. They tend to merge at a point, yet they maintain their own distinctive characteristics. Let me talk about their distinctive characteristics and, hopefully, you will let the Bible permit them to merge now and then and use them interchangeably.

Mercy

Mercy is the withholding of judgement when you have it in your power to bring judgement upon somebody, when it is within the scope of your authority. For instance, you're whizzing down the M6, and you're up around ninety miles an hour. You look in your rear view mirror and here comes one of those wonderful gentlemen that helps keep the peace in the UK. He pulls you over and has the power and authority to bring immediate judgement on your life. He walks up, you roll down your window and he reminds you of your sin and you agree. Then you give him that longing look and he takes pity and says, 'You seem to be a pretty nice person so slow down and let's forget the ticket.'

Technically that would be mercy because he has withheld the judgement that he has the appropriate authority to exercise. Would it have been a loving thing for him to do? Of course. Would it have been a gracious thing for him to do? Of course. But, technically, that's mercy.

Love

Love is probably the broadest, most general word, especially if you're talking about the *agape* love of the almighty God and Jesus Christ. That unconditional choice, regardless of the environment, to see a need and give our resources to meet a need; probably the most general of all the words.

Grace

Grace, in its technical distinction, is when, in the face of someone who deserves something bad back from you, you withhold what they deserve. In the face of what is not fair, you could give somebody what they deserve. But grace withholds what they deserve and blesses them in spite of what they might deserve.

The application of grace

Now, these words do flow together. For instance, Ephesians chapter 5, the leading command to husbands is 'Love your wives even as Christ loved the church and gave himself'. 'For by grace are you saved, through faith.' It's not of yourself. There's a place where love and grace and mercy merge; the cross wraps up all three of them. It withholds the judgement that is due me, I am undeserving of it and it is an act of his love. All three of these merge wonderfully in the cross. I think it's critical, when you move forward in the application of grace, that you understand some of these distinctives between mercy and love and grace.

Grace in the face of wrongdoing

How do you deal with grace in the face of wrongdoing? Does it mean you're a doormat? We mentioned yesterday that the Bible has a pattern of what you do when there is wrongdoing. Galatians 6:1 is very clear: you see a brother or sister caught in sin, you ought to go to them but make sure you go with the right attitude. In fact, doesn't the Bible say we should speak the truth in love? So often getting in the face of wrongdoing is not the act but the attitude that we do it with.

Church discipline, which is a biblical requirement of a local New Testament church, is an act of grace because it confronts somebody with a wrong. What is the purpose of church discipline? Restoration; resolution of the issue, that's a mark of grace. Prophetic preaching, making sin clear, is an act of grace because there is no acceptance of grace until first you know you need grace. Francis Schaeffer said it so well: 'If we ever speak clearly about sin and the judgement of God, we must learn to do it with tears running down our cheeks.' I don't want three thousand of us leaving here and suddenly forgetting about the fact that there is a ministry of prophetic utterance about sin and righteousness. But grace must always cradle it in an attitude that urges people from that sin, to come to the wonderful and forgiving grace of Jesus Christ.

Grace is not the standard for unity

If we think 'We must be gracious to everybody, regardless of their doctrinal persuasions. Grace is the foundation for unity' – go to John chapter 17. Jesus Christ has a very interesting developmental flow in that high priestly prayer. The first thing he said is, 'Lord sanctify them through thy truth.' So it is the truth of God, the non-negotiable authoritative truth of God that sets us apart as a group. Truth defines our unity.

Then he says, 'That they may be one.' After the truth defines us, then within that truth, we are one and that's our testimony to Jesus Christ. Grace then flows out of that body unity to everybody, regardless. I get concerned because I see a lot of this fuzzy thinking about. Everybody's included because we want to be nice people. I had a lady come to me. She said, 'My neighbour's a Mormon and we pray together, every day.' I think that Mormons ought to be objects of every ounce of grace that I have but Mormons don't believe that Jesus Christ is the almighty God. We dare never let the whole issue of grace blur the truth because as soon as the church loses the truth, it has nothing left to bring to this culture. More specifically, in this situation, if we make the fact that Jesus is God secondary, we have no salvation to bring to the culture.

Grace is an attitude

I gave you the definition that grace is an action. Well, actually grace, before it ever becomes an action, is an attitude, looking for a place to happen. You have to get up in the morning ready to do grace, looking for a place to do grace. It begins as an attitude, waiting to flow into somebody's life. The book of John is like a photo album, picture after picture of Jesus in action. So if it is true that the purpose of the prologue is to prepare us for the book and if a major section of the prologue is on the fact that Jesus extended grace as a reflection of the glory of God, we ought to expect that some of the snapshots in the album ought to be about that. Let Jesus teach us grace applied, by watching his life, that we might be like him.

Eight snapshots

I want to take you through eight snapshots in the book of John. We're going to begin in verse 16: 'For of his fullness we have all received...' Grace is all inclusive, nobody is exempt.

Now, I think it's important, when you read the Bible, to stop on words and say: 'what does "all" mean?' Let me take you to the snapshot of the 'all' that he's talking about. I would think that it probably meant anybody was touched by his grace but, more specifically, given what happens in the rest of this chapter, he's talking about the disciples first and foremost.

Snapshot 1: Grace is all-inclusive

Did you ever think about the disciples and the kind of people they were?

Peter – Let's start with Peter, who's the punching bag. He has lot of good qualities we ought to track once in a while. Peter did have some idiosyncrasies – always spouting off, always, 'I'll do that Lord.' and rarely following through. Do you know anybody like that? Do they bother you sometimes?

Andrew – Andrew, his brother, doesn't say a whole lot in the New Testament. At one point, in feeding the five thousand, Andrew brings this little boy with this lunch. Then he says, 'Lord, we did find a little food' and then he makes it 'but what are these among so many?' After Jesus had been healing the lame and making the blind to see… Andrew, if you get one quote in the Bible – not that one! He hardly ever says anything. Have you ever been around quiet people? Do quiet people bother you? They bother me! 'What are you thinking? Talk to me!' Of course, if you grew up with Peter as a brother, you'd be quiet too. You'd never have a chance to say anything in your whole life!

James and John – James and John were nicknamed 'sons of thunder'. 'John, would you please get your act together?' He's always the mushy one – even in the epistles. Read 1 John and it's love: he's the one leaning on Jesus' bosom and yet he's got this temper problem. At one point he and his brother want to call down lightning on the enemies of Jesus Christ. 'You're such a split personality! I get used to you this way and all of a sudden you're this way!' You been around people like that?

Thomas, the sceptic – If you ever throw a party, don't ever invite a sceptic. They go around going, 'Oh yeah, prove it.' Then, when it falls apart, they're going 'I told you so.'

Matthew – He has to be totally despised by the rest of these guys because he was a tax collector. The reason these guys were so hated was that they had sold themselves out to the Roman government. The Roman government was the oppressing army that had robbed Israel of its glory and grandeur and they were under the decadent Roman empire. A few of these Jewish guys, for personal gain, worked for the Roman government, collecting taxes, total traitors! Not only that, it was a common practice for them to add a few of their own assessments to the tax rate and stick it in their back pocket. People hated tax collectors.

Simon the Zealot – There was Matthew; now there's a little extra tension because you have Simon the Zealot. He was committed to the resistance force, to overthrow the Roman empire, willing to spill blood on the streets, walking around in military fatigues and an Uzi over his shoulder. He's in the group – with Matthew.

Jesus had an interesting crew here. I want to ask you this question: do you think Jesus always liked everything they did and everything about them? No. Do you think Jesus was willing and ready, in a moment's notice, to extend his grace to each of them? Yes. And Judas is included in the list. For three years Judas was an object of the grace of God. If you want to begin applying this snapshot to your life, please don't wait to do grace for the people you like. Grace is all inclusive. It is to be extended to everyone who crosses the path of your existence.

Snapshot 2: Grace is always generous

I love the fact that the very first story told about Christ is that he goes to a party. I think that's wonderful for all of us who think that Jesus was this extremely holy serious guy who never went out much. He shows up at the wedding feast of Cana and he finds out, through his mother, that they've run out of wine. I'm not going to get into a fight over whether this was grape juice or wine. That is not relevant to the snapshot. I have my own opinion on that but I don't want to get myself in trouble.

He could have walked away, he could have said 'It's none of my business. It's not my moment.' But even though it wasn't his moment or necessarily his business, he stayed. He could have said, 'They're out of wine. Who's the knuckle-head that planned this party? He had the guest list. There's no way that I'm letting this guy off the hook. He'll never learn his lesson and he'll do this every time he throws a wedding party.' Jesus didn't think that. Or Jesus might have thought, 'I've come to display the grace of God on this planet, to help in time of need. They certainly don't deserve it and that party manager does not deserve it. But we'll do a grace thing here. Do a head count; we'll do one glass apiece because I've got three years ahead of me, I can't spend all my grace at the first party I go to.' Do you know how much wine he provided? Three thousand, five hundred, six ounce glasses of wine, wow! Just to prove that grace is generous. There is a generosity of grace that overwhelms people's lives.

Think of your resources, think of your power, think of your energies, think of all that you have. Are you stingy with those? Would you rather find fault with other people so you can horde them to yourselves? Or would you extend your spiritual gifts and teach young kids in your church? Would you break out your cheque book? Give sacrificially to the kingdom of Jesus Christ or are you trying to save it all for yourself? The Bible has a lot to say about that. But it's not about money. It begins, I believe, in a generosity of spirit. Where grace is generous in spirit, it's willing to cut people a little slack now and then. The generosity of grace gives people a little space. How many of you wish that people would give you a little space in your life? I find that the grace of generosity of spirit comes particularly hard driving. I'm a type A person and I'm a type A person when I drive and I'm not proud. I'm working on it. I'm trying to transition toward more grace here. But I'm so competitive.

We need to get the point: when Jesus poured out his grace, it was generous. Do you know what Paul says about his grace to you in your time of need? If God brings something into your life, his grace will be sufficient. I like what F.B. Meyers said when he wrote his commentary on Psalm 23. He says 'God is not a stingy God.' In the verse on the overflowing cup, he said 'With God, it is always the overflowing cup, it is the fatted calf, it is the best robe, it is the best ring. Our God is a generous God.' And we walk around this planet, thinking we're like Jesus, glorifying God and being hoarding and stingy with all our resources. We are not like Christ and that is not what grace is about because grace is generous, by its very nature. If you wonder about how much grace you ought to give, figure it out and then give a little bit more to make sure.

Snapshot 3: Grace dissolves prejudice

We have to go to chapter four where Jesus meets the woman at the well. In the King James, John chapter four begins with him saying to his disciples, 'We must needs go home through Samaria.' Now, any Jew worth their Torah never went home through Samaria. They literally, geographically, could go around and they would often take their journey around, to go back to Jerusalem and avoid going through Samaria. Why? Because the Samaritans were the enemies of the Jews. This was no recent political fire storm; this had been for centuries they had hated each other. They had ransacked each others' temples, they had a heritage of ethnic, cultural rivalry, exploding in a flat out hatred for each other. If you were a Jewish parent, you would say to your children, 'Don't you ever play with a Samaritan child, I don't want to catch you playing with a Samaritan child.' The Samaritans would do the same. What a shock to the disciples! I love Jesus because he is so full of surprises. An adventure with Jesus is always out on the edge.

He says, 'We're going home through Samaria.' I'll tell you one reason they needed to go through Samaria: they needed to learn a lesson of grace. 'I want to take you through Samaria, because there are people who live around you, who aren't like you, part of ethnic subcultures that you don't like.' Reigning in the hearts of even the most consecrated of us is this enemy called pride, waiting to devour our capacity to be like Jesus Christ.

So let's walk with them. They go into town to buy a meal. Jesus is so exhausted from the journey that he sits by the well. Who came along? A woman. Big problem for a Rabbi: in that culture, Rabbis had nothing to do with women. You were never seen, in public, with a woman, ever! Literature tells us that if a Rabbi was walking down the street and a woman was coming, he'd go to the other side of the street till the woman had got by and then resume his journey. They were sources of seduction and so it never happened. For him to stay there, with this woman, was a high risk to his credibility and claim to be God and credibility as a teacher.

We learned yesterday that grace will take you into relationships that are risky. This was a high risk for him. Any Rabbi would have left: he stayed. Not only does the text tell us it was a woman but it was a woman of Samaria. So there you have ethnic, cultural problems. The text doesn't tell us until later, but Jesus knew very well that she was not only a woman of Samaria, but she was known as an immoral woman of Samaria. And Jesus stayed. Grace will consistently urge you to the point of dissolving your pride and your prejudices and your assumptions. It will tear down the normal cultural barriers that we erect to keep us from people who aren't like ourselves, because grace is inclusive of everybody, as we have already learned. He goes beyond the fault of her personal profile to her need, that's what grace does. He told her that he was the Messiah, and, where as she could draw water that would expire, he could give her water that would never expire in her soul. She runs into the city and she tells all of her friends, probably some of her ex-husbands, 'I think I've found the real Messiah.' Here these guys are coming out and women and revival's broken out. There was cheering in heaven.

Enter the disciples; they come back with lunch. See if you are more like them or like Jesus. They come walking back and, from a distance, they see him with the woman and the text says that they were extremely distraught that Jesus would be at this well, with this woman. They are murmuring among themselves. This isn't in the text but they've got to be saying something like, 'What is he doing? Doesn't he know he's going to wreck everything? People are related in Jerusalem, word will get back.' But they're such wimps. The text says, 'but they didn't say anything to Jesus.' Except 'Sir, here is your lunch.' And he said, 'I have food to eat that you know not of.' He was saying 'I am so caught in this grace transaction, I am so overwhelmed, I'm so satisfied and fulfilled in extending the grace of eternal life to this woman, I don't even want to eat.' But they are so clueless, so unplugged, so wrapped into their material world of lunches and prejudice and cultural differences, that they say to each other, 'Did somebody bring him something to eat?'

Then he sat them down and he taught them and then he said to them, 'Look out onto the fields, for they are white indeed, unto the harvest, we need workers to go.' We don't mind sending missionaries to other kinds of people, we're bothered when other kinds of people move next door. As a pastor, this guy came to me and he said, 'Pastor, do you have any follow-up material I could use with a neighbour of mine? About six months ago, we had some new people move in next door, and they were Indian. So as soon as they moved in, my wife and I decided, "God has brought the mission field to our neighbourhood, we're going to start praying for these people, maybe we can lead them to the Lord.'" I know a lot of Christians who would peek through the blinds and go, 'Oh my goodness, there goes the neighbourhood. Call the estate agent.' He said, 'Last night, the lady in that home accepted Christ in our living room and we want to make sure we track with her.' The grace that dissolves prejudice and cultural barriers: what a marvellous snapshot for us.

I was in a church near Chicago and I was preaching, last summer and in the worship time, I noticed across the aisle, in the front row, this young lady in a white dress, with short sleeves. What took my attention was a big tattoo, running all the way down her left arm. My first impulse, I'm ashamed to tell you, was 'What is she doing here? I bet she's feeling embarrassed. If she'd looked in the mirror, she probably would have worn a long sleeved shirt.' She had her hands up praising God, deep in the worship of the Jesus that she loved. And as I have this horrible, non-grace, prejudicial, culturally bound attitude going, the Holy Spirit grabbed me, threw me to the floor, put his foot on my chest and said, 'Stowell, you think you're so cool. What do you think God thinks of you when he extends his grace to you? You got sin tattoos all over your soul and look what he did for you.' I realised that probably that tattoo is a mark of her life before she came to Jesus. I was so ashamed because I refused, in my heart, to cover her with the same grace that Jesus had covered her with and I knew how wrong I had been.

Snapshot 4: Grace helps the helpless

John chapter 5 the man who is at the well. Jesus walks by him, in verse 6, and says, 'Do you wish to get to the well?' And the sick man answered him 'Sir, I have no man to put me into the pool, when the water is stirred.' Here is a helpless person, totally unable to be healed and desperately needing someone. Think about him, lying there for all those years, everybody walking by and no one has ever said what Jesus said to him. Nobody cared. Our world is full of people who are hopeless and helpless, who desperately need a touch of grace from us. Jesus said, 'I'll help you.'

I have a pastor friend in Minneapolis, Minnesota, who's recognised as a leader on biblical church leadership and church growth and I have a friend who works on his staff. I said to him one time, 'What's it like to work with him?' He said, 'We come into meetings and we throw something on the table and his first response always is, "What can we do to help?"' Jesus takes this man, he says, 'I'll help you.' And he graces him and he is healed. That's an important snapshot. We live in a world of helpless people. And I'm disabled here because I'm so stuck in the States for most of my perspectives and experiences and mind-set. We have a lot of problem people in the States. The normal philosophy runs, 'These poor people are victims. Let me tell you about their mother. If they didn't have the kind of mother they had, they probably could be rather decent citizens.' Everybody gets off the hook because everybody is a victim.

I know a lot of Christians who are going, 'Don't give me that victim talk. Get up, make something of yourself, get a job.' Do you ever hear that? Do you ever think that? I want you to know there are some true victims in this world. I minister on the Moody campus, twenty-three acres stuck right in the heart of the great city of Chicago. Blocks away is Carbine Green. Blocks away, the other way, is the Gold Coast, one of the richest housing sections in the world. And over in Carbine Green, every single day there are little babies born to crack mums, without a father. That's a victim, by no choice of their own. Birmingham, Manchester, Leeds, London, you name it, a town near you, somewhere there are people who have been born into horrid straits and they truly are victims and desperately need somebody to help them. Grace reaches out to help the helpless.

May God give you the pleasure, some time, of being somewhere, near somebody, lying by the side of a well, with no help, waiting for a touch of grace, that you could come and help the helpless. Jesus came to help the helpless and you and I were helpless, in our sin. Hopelessly lying by a well and no one to give us salvation, until Jesus came. And, if he helped me in my helpless, hopeless state, should I not be looking, today, for somebody who is helpless, that I might help. That's the grace of Jesus.

Chapter 5
The characteristics of grace

Introduction

Yesterday we opened up the album of the book of John to see snapshots of Jesus, doing grace in action. Remember, this isn't some kind of passive exercise, this is about being committed to becoming like Christ, that we might glorify God. So these snapshots, in the book of John, actually become targets for me, for my life and your life, a list of ways in which you can start doing grace.

Snapshot 5: Grace is never put off by man's traditions

Open your Bibles to John 5, we'll go to the fifth snapshot. Let's begin at verse 8. 'Jesus said to him, "Arise, take up your pallet and walk" and immediately the man became well and took up his pallet and began to walk.' Let me urge you not to read your Bibles quickly. Could you imagine this moment? This man has been lying there for years hoping. He can't walk, his limbs are withered and Jesus speaks and he walks. Can you get a grip on that?

Verse 10, 'the Jews were saying to him, who was cured, "Hey, don't you know that it is the Sabbath? It is not permissible for you to carry your pallet."' Jesus has just done such a glorious act, you'd think that the

Jews would be striking up the band. But instead they're locked into this. There's a very important issue here: grace is never put off by the traditions and rules of men, be careful of that. Who said it wasn't lawful to carry your pallet on the Sabbath? God said, 'You should keep the Sabbath holy.' Which means distinct, other, sacred. I think what Jesus did was distinct, other, sacred. God just said, 'Keep it holy.' Did God want to depreciate this guy's assets, by forcing him to leave the pallet behind?

The reason they're so upset is because Jesus is coming out against the traditions of the Pharisees. He's trying to make a point that God gave the law, which is absolute authority, which grace does not obliterate: grace always works within the context of righteousness, what is right. What they did, with the law of God, was extrapolate out applications of the law. For the Sabbath, they had a multiplicity of very complex applications of the law. The problem was what they did making their applications of equal weight with the law of God, so that the applications of righteousness carried divine authority. That's why Jesus said, 'Your traditions oppress the people.' For those who have been in the church a long time, you might think that strictness is next to godliness. It is possible to be more strict than God and that is being ungodly because it is not like God.

Relevant applications of the law are often wise but we dare never give them equal weight with the law. Please beware that your grace is not inhibited by man-made rules and traditions. If God calls you to be a missionary to bikers and you say, 'It's really not godly to have a ponytail and an earring and it's not godly to wear leather all the time. The people in my church would be upset about that and then I wouldn't get any missionary support. . .' forget it! Go get the bikers, don't do what they do all the time because that would break the law but do everything you can to bring grace to them, don't let man-made rules inhibit grace. True grace is not put off by the traditions and man-made rules of men.

Snapshot 6: Grace gives a second chance

In John chapter 8 we meet the woman taken in adultery. Jesus is in the crowd and the Pharisees, constantly wanting to trip him up, come and say 'Sir, we found this woman committing adultery.'

Before we go any farther, you have to ask yourself; where's the guy?
It takes two to commit adultery. I think this lady could have been set
up as an opportunity for them to embarrass Christ; otherwise you'd
have both the people there. The Pharisees were willing to do anything
just to get Jesus. What was really behind this?

Jesus only had two options: answer number one, the law said that
she should be stoned. The problem is nobody was stoned for adultery
any more, in that day. So, if Jesus said, 'The law says stone her', then he
loses all credibility with the crowd. If he says, 'Let her off' then the
Pharisees can say, 'He claims to be God and on this he's a law breaker.'
He's stuck; this is a really huge set-up. Jesus doesn't answer them. He
writes in the sand and then he says, to these guys, 'He who is without
sin, you pick up the first stone.' You've got to be divine to come up
with an answer like that!' And they're going, 'I'm out of here.'

He's left alone with the woman and writes with his finger, the text
is clear about that, in the sand a second time. Writing with your finger once then twice, can you think of any reference point in
Scripture? Exodus 33 and 34, where God gave the law. Moses went
and saw the rebellion of the people, worshipping the pagan calf. He
breaks the tablets, comes back and says, 'God, what do you do in a
moment like this? I need to know your ways.' God says, 'Make two
more tablets of stone.' And he wrote the law again, because he is a God
of second chances. You say, 'But you don't want to let people off the
hook.' He didn't; he then turned and said 'Go thy way and sin no
more.' The God of the second chance, that's what grace is. Try it in
your world.

Snapshot 7: Grace goes beyond analysis to meet the needs

Chapter nine: as Jesus walks by, the disciples stop him and say 'Lord,
here is this man born blind. He's been here for years.' I would have
thought the disciples, had they started to get a grip on grace, would
have said, 'Lord, heal him.' That's how slow we are to get a grip on
grace. So they say, 'Lord wait, we've been having discussions about this
particular individual, and we're having a very serious problem getting
clarity on a couple of issues about his blindness. Why was he born
blind? Could it be that he sinned in his mother's womb?' (Or, just to

bring us up to Keswick 2003, you see somebody suddenly have some massive illness or tragedy in their family. One of the first things that flashes through your brain, perhaps, is, 'I wonder if they're being disciplined by God for some major sin in their life?') They say, 'Or, perhaps Lord, could it be that his parents sinned and God is judging him for his parents' sin? Maybe you could help us with this theological problem.'

It's always 'let's analyse this problem; obviously somebody did something really bad for this guy to be born blind.' No thought of grace, no thought of getting beyond that stuff to find the need and take the resources of your life, under the power of the Holy Spirit, to touch some, metaphorically speaking, blind person. The grace of God gets you beyond analysis and fault finding and curiosity about people's problems and takes you to help them.

Then Jesus said, 'This man was not born blind for any of those reasons but he was born blind that my Father might be glorified.' There it is again, the whole link; grace in action bringing glory to God because God is a God of grace. Jesus got beyond all that and made the blind to see so that people would say, 'Your claim to be God must be true. Is this what God is like?'

When you touch somebody with grace, don't get caught in this trap, because sometimes there will be a little smattering of applause. Don't ever rob God of his glory, it's a very serious thing. Nebuchadnezzar, who robbed God of his glory, was banished, as an animal, to eat in the field. If you touch somebody with grace and you get the opportunity to interact with them, please tell them that it is not of you. Say, 'I love you but I wouldn't have known about this if I hadn't met Jesus and this is all about him. If you feel touched, thank God, you've been touched by God.' This man was born blind, that God might be glorified.

Snapshot 8: The grace of forgiveness

This is, perhaps, the most challenging target of grace that any of us will ever experience. It is forgiving those who've offended us, all the way to the very worst, unspeakable offences in our lives. You get to John 12 and he is opening the section of his album that you and I would call the cross. And from John 12 through the twentieth chapter, John spends the majority of his book in the cross narrative.

Think about the fact that you have been touched by the grace, the forgiveness, of God. You say, 'I'm really quite a good person so actually he didn't have much to forgive.' Is that your theology? That Jesus came to die for good people? Have you not clearly seen yourself, before a holy, perfect God? Have you not known how deeply offensive the very best of us have been to a holy God? How your sins have touched him to the core? How he has grieved over you? How he has been hurt by you and yet, in spite of all of that, he forgave you?

Someone has said that the banner over the kingdom of Jesus Christ reads: forgiveness. It is the leading issue of the kingdom of Jesus Christ, it's how people get into the kingdom, it's how people express their difference as people of the kingdom. How, therefore, can we call ourselves followers of the King when we do not even exercise the most fundamental, most significant, strategic aspect of the kingdom in forgiving others as we have been forgiven?

I want to give you five pointers from the Bible on forgiveness because it's very complex. Some of you have been deeply offended, maybe for years, by a parent, in unspeakable ways. Some have been betrayed by a close friend, some abandoned by a spouse. Some have deep hurts so I don't want to minimise this. I just want to turn your face to the liberty and the wonderful grace of forgiveness and maybe I can get you started so that you can know the joy of it all.

The importance of forgiveness – I want to remind you of the importance of forgiveness, on a practical scale, for you as a person. Richard Holloway, in his book called *On forgiveness*,[1] writes, 'even though it may seem morally appropriate, refusing to forgive always extends the reign of the original sin into the future so that it ends up dominating our entire life or even the life of whole people or of a family.'

That is so profound. Refusal to forgive extends the impact of the original sin. You carry it with you for the rest of your life. You see all of life through it, you treat other people through it. I am reminded of

---

[1]   Richard Holloway, *On Forgiveness* (Edinburgh: Canongate, 2002)

Hebrews where we read beware of bitterness because if you let a root of bitterness grow up within you, many will be defiled. The power of the lack of forgiveness gives that original offence the power to keep you stuck in the past.

In another place he writes

> When true forgiveness happens, it is one of the most astonishing and liberating of the human experiences. The tragedy of the many ways we trespass upon each other is that we can damage people, so deeply that we can rob them of the future by stopping the movement of their lives at the moment of the injury, which continues to send out shock waves of pain, that swamp their whole existence... Forgiveness, when it happens, is able to move that dead weight from our past and give us back our lives again.[2]

There are very deep, practical ramifications to people who refuse to forgive, but more serious than that is what the Bible says. Matthew chapter 5:43 and 48, 'Jesus said "You have heard it said you should love your friends and hate your enemies."' That was the normal proverb of the day. 'But I say unto you', get the transition, from normal living unto kingdom living. Any time Jesus says, in the Gospels, 'but I say unto you', you ought to sit up and pay attention because he's trying to yank you out of the fallenness that we normally live in, into the wonder of being kingdom people. He said, 'but I say unto you, you should love your enemies, bless those who curse you, pray for those who despitefully use you.' Here's why forgiveness is so important, 'so that you may be like your Father in heaven, who has forgiven you.'

Please do not claim to be on the pilgrimage to becoming like Christ if you resolutely resolve, in your heart, not to forgive. Jesus made this clear in another passage. 'Please don't ask me to forgive you if you have been unwilling to forgive others.' You cannot minimise the biblical importance of starting on the journey of forgiving those who have offended you. And nobody can fully forgive unless you've been forgiven by Jesus, that's part of why it's the banner of the kingdom. Nobody forgives regardless, except those who have been

---

[2] Richard Holloway, *On Forgiveness* (Edinburgh: Canongate 2002)

touched by Jesus Christ, you just can't do it. That's why it makes it such a powerful testimony.

The motivation for forgiveness – Some of you are saying, 'But they don't deserve it.' You're exactly right, they don't deserve it. Forgiveness does not focus on the fault doer. Get vertical, that's the problem with our lives, we're so totally horizontal. We're vertical people, we do things because God asks us to do them. You forgive even the worst offender, because God asked you. You do it for him, you don't do it for them. You do it because you want to reflect the glory of Christ. Does Jesus deserve your forgiveness of your enemy? Yes; absolutely, he deserves it.

You say, 'But this person doesn't even want my forgiveness.' It doesn't make any difference if they deserve or want it, we do it because we're followers of Christ, that God might be glorified.

The timing of forgiveness – You say 'If they ask for it, I'll give it to them.' Let me ask you an interesting question. When did Jesus forgive you? I didn't ask when was your forgiveness in Jesus actualised? When did he forgive you? Two thousand years ago, he spread his arms in a posture of full, unconditional forgiveness. Today is the day that you begin to forgive your enemies. If God begins to work in their lives and they come to you and say, 'Would you please forgive me?', say 'I already have.'

If you're going to be like Jesus, remember that grace is an attitude that leads to an action. You forgive now, don't wait till they come. If you wait till they come, bitterness and all those bad things will continue to do their damage. They may never come. Start it now. God had the posture of forgiveness in eternity past, it's an eternal thing with the almighty God.

The confidence to forgive – You need a little confidence that will release you to forgive and the confidence is built on two things. No matter how deep the trouble was, God means it for good. Read the life of Joseph. From this dysfunctional family, doing everything his daddy tells him to, his brothers hate him, they try to kill him, they sell him as a slave into Egypt, ends up three years in prison, talk about bitterness. Finally they show up in his court so who's got the power now?

Joseph's testimony has to be the testimony of your heart. He said, 'You guys meant it for evil: God meant it for good.'

Every offence in your life is permitted by a holy God. He stands as the sovereign sentinel at your gate. He won't permit anything in that he can't turn to his glory, the gain of his kingdom and the ultimate good of your life. You have to see your enemies as the hand of God, maybe the surgical tool. Read James chapter 1. This is not a random hit, that you got all of a sudden by fate, it was done by the permission of God because God has a much bigger plan for you. And whereas that person meant it for evil, God ultimately means it for good. Can you get a grip on that? That's a confidence that will begin to give you the liberty to forgive.

Secondly, you say, 'But they're going to get off scot free.' Romans chapter 12, says, 'Live at peace with all men, put wrath in its proper place, for vengeance is mine.' Give your enemies to God. Let God take care of your enemies: that's the confidence.

Turn your enemies around – The energy that keeps bitterness from creeping back in again is your positive commitment to turn around, in love, your enemies. If you do not trigger the power of love to your enemy, after you have moved to a point of forgiveness, the bile of that bitterness will seep back in. You need to be exercising what Jesus did for us, he forgave us and loves us, even when we still hurt him. You'll struggle with it all over again.

You say, 'But they don't want to have anything to do with me.' Fine, pray for them every day, God will touch their lives. That'll be the true test of forgiveness. 'Dear Lord, help Bob, who I've hated deeply in the past, to have a really good day today.' The only way you can do that is if you've given him to the Lord; that frees you up to love your enemy, take him lunch, write him a note. If they keep saying 'Don't ever talk to me again,' just pray for them, every day.

Grace has to be intentional

Almost half the book is about the grace of forgiveness and my guess is probably all of us can use this as a target. Be intentional about this whole grace project. This won't happen if you don't commit yourself to it. Get up every morning and say, 'Lord, please give me an opportunity to become like you and to glorify your name by touching someone with your grace; with an act of abundant kindness, regardless, even to the most undeserving offender.'

Last summer I was out early in the morning, running. I'd told Marty that I'd bring her a cup of coffee when I came home and so I stopped at Starbucks. It was 6.30 in the morning, they had just opened up and I'm the second guy in line. The guy in front of me was having this real knockdown with the clerk and he's going, 'I want this *New York Times*. I got a fifty dollar bill here, what do you mean you don't have change?' The clerk's going, 'I'm really sorry, but we don't have change for a fifty dollar bill.'

So, all of a sudden, I realise, 'An opportunity for the generosity of grace to somebody so undeserving.' I said to the clerk, 'I'll pay for his paper. Just put it on my bill. Seventy-five cents is no big deal. Take the paper, have a great day.'

He walks out, he's going, 'Wow, everything I have is yours.' Which obviously didn't include the fifty dollar bill... But I didn't expect to have happen what happened next because as the clerk gave me my coffee, he said, 'That was a really nice thing you did. Our world would be a lot better place if there were more people like you.'

Now, I knew that our world probably wouldn't be a lot better place if people were like me but it was 6.30, I was tired from my run. I think I have a platform here to say something. I think God has used grace to build the platform. And nothing came. I still pray for that clerk and I pray that he gets around a lot of us Bible people. And every time he's around us, he beholds the grace, until he finally comes and asks, 'What is it that you people have?' Then we can tell him about Jesus.

I've been in a lot of meetings where the Spirit of God has spoken to my heart. Then I go home and it's back to business as usual. I want to fight against what Jesus talked about in that parable of the soils and the seeds because the tares grow up and choke the seeds. He defines the tares as the cares and riches of this world. It is Satan's desire now, in your heart, to spring the tares and to choke out what God has spoken to your heart.

Do you love me?

Would you turn all the way to John 21? Jesus has risen and he has the last exchange with Peter, and he says to Peter, verse 15, 'Simon, son of John, do you love me more than these?' Peter said, 'Yes Lord, you know that I love you.' And he said, 'Then tend my lambs.' You're thinking, 'This is a verse for pastors.' Tending lambs is giving yourself to the needs and nurture of people. That your life is focused on the needs and nurture of people, that's a grace concept. Grace always moves to meet a need, to nurture people.

Peter said, 'You know that I love you.' Jesus is saying, 'I'll know you love me when you care about people.' Jesus knows you love him when you care about what he cares about. That's the principle. Jesus came and was passionately addicted to one commodity on this planet and that was people and their needs. The scary thing for me, doing what I do, is that I suddenly realise I can be busy, busy, for Jesus and he never feels loved by me because I have not dedicated myself to the needs and nurture of people. How quickly we become distracted by lesser stuff or even by ourselves. Jesus has a love language and you touch him with your love when you care about what he cares about, gracing the needs and nurture of people.

Why did Jesus ask, 'Do you love me?' What's the issue in these texts? Go to the context, back up to verse 3 of chapter 21. Peter was with a whole group of the disciples and he says to them, 'I'm going fishing.' And they say 'Good, we'll go with you.'

What's going on there? Is that a day off? I don't think Jesus would have a problem with a day off. Even Jesus went apart and rested a while. There's only one other thing that this could be. Peter was saying, 'I'm going back to business as usual.' Because for three intensive years he has expected that Jesus would become the king, overthrow Rome, establish his throne and Peter would be in the Cabinet and everything was going to be glorious. Then there's this crashing disappointment that Jesus goes to the cross. Then the joy of the resurrection but, as the text tells us, this is only the third time Jesus has shown up, it's not like it used to be. Jesus shows up in weird ways, materialises from behind closed doors and talks to them, shows his wounds and eats and he's gone. Peter is deeply discouraged.

Keep going!

Here's the point that I would like to make. You will go home and you'll begin this grace journey and Satan's going to put something in front of you and you are going to be discouraged. And you are going to say, 'It's just not turning out the way I thought it would.' I think that's exactly where Peter is. His expectations are dashed. Maybe he needed a little money because Judas has absconded with the treasury. So he's going to stop trusting Jesus to provide for him. And he goes off mission, off calling, off the grace route. And all the other disciples say, 'Let's open up a new business.' Then they fished all night; they catch nothing. Then Jesus showed up on the shore, and they have no idea who this guy is and he goes 'You catching anything?' Jesus never asks a question because he doesn't know the answer, he always asks questions to make a point. And they're going, 'No, we didn't catch anything.'

'Oh,' he said. 'Well, take your nets, throw them on the other side of the boat.' They're going, 'Who does he think he is? We've been fishing all night out here.' Maybe somebody said, 'Let's try.' They throw it over and they can't even pull it in, there are so many fish. John goes, 'It must be the Lord.' And suddenly they know it's the Lord and Peter does this Peter thing. He grabs his robe, jumps overboard, sloshes to the shore and there's Jesus.

Why did Peter do that? Because this was not some incidental, random thought that Jesus had, to do the net on the other side of the boat thing. Do any of you remember the other time that happened? It was Luke chapter 5. Peter left his nets and followed Christ, until John 21 when, because of the discouragement and the difficulties that he faced, he goes off mission, off calling and Jesus meets him on the shore and says, 'Peter, I need you.' You and I sit here, redeemed, because those eleven guys stuck with it. Because they didn't give up. Jesus called him back on mission again and got him going in the right direction.

I say that to remind you that you will feel very discouraged at times with this grace project. Don't go off calling, don't go off mission, don't go off vision. Jesus has called you to follow him, to be an instrument of grace.

Now, I understand why Jesus said, 'Peter, do you love me more than fish?' What are the fish in your life that deter and distract you from this holy calling of God to be an instrument of grace, to move to the needs and nurture of people? Is it someone's large offence? Is it that your career is more important? Is it that you have other dreams? Is it that you have a secret sin? I don't know what will distract and discourage you, I just want Jesus to keep showing up on the beach of your life until you get all the way home, to heaven, calling you back, saying, 'I need you.' It might be for you to anchor down July 18th 2003, as the moment he showed up on the beach, to call you afresh to this mission.

The thing that strikes me most is that when the disciples came to the shore, Jesus had a charcoal fire burning. Why is that detail in the narrative? The word charcoal is only used one other place in Scripture; in the New Testament, when Peter was in the outer courts, seated at a charcoal fire. Aromas bring back memories. Peter comes up on the shore and that pungent aroma of a charcoal fire had to remind him, just a few days earlier, that he was a failure. Jesus needs those who fail him. That's no excuse to fail but it is to say that your failures, on the journey, are not a reason for you not to get back up and follow him in spite of the failures. He's on the beach calling you to follow him, to be like him. This is our commitment, together, to be followers of Christ, all the way, to touching our world with his grace.

The Addresses

Pitfalls and Hazards in Discipleship I
by Angus MacLeay

ANGUS MacLEAY

Converted whilst at Oxford University where he was reading law, Angus qualified as a solicitor before becoming curate of Holy Trinity Platt from 1988-1992. He then became vicar of Houghton with Kingmoor in Carlisle for nine years before moving south to St Nicholas in Sevenoaks, Kent, where he is now Rector. His hobbies include walking, climbing, reading and playing a good game of hockey!

Pitfalls and Hazards in Discipleship I

Introduction

Let's turn to Philippians chapter 2 and we're going to be reading from chapter 2 and verses 1-18.

> If you have any encouragement from being united with Christ, if any comfort from his love, if any fellowship with the Spirit, if any tenderness and compassion, then make my joy complete by being like-minded, having the same love, being one in spirit and purpose. Do nothing out of selfish ambition or vain conceit, but in humility consider others better than yourselves. Each of you should look not only to your own interests, but also to the interests of others. Your attitude should be the same as that of Christ Jesus:
> Who, being in very nature God,
> did not consider equality with God something to be grasped,
> but made himself nothing,
> taking the very nature of a servant,
> being made in human likeness.
> And being found in appearance as a man,
> he humbled himself
> and became obedient to death – even death on a cross!
> Therefore God exalted him to the highest place

and gave him the name that is above every name,
that at the name of Jesus every knee should bow,
in heaven and on earth and under the earth,
and every tongue confess that Jesus Christ is Lord,
to the glory of God the Father.

Therefore, my dear friends, as you have always obeyed – not only in my presence, but now much more in my absence – continue to work out your salvation with fear and trembling, for it is God who works in you to will and to act according to his good purpose.

Do everything without complaining or arguing, so that you may become blameless and pure, children of God without fault in a crooked and depraved generation, in which you shine like stars in the universe as you hold out the word of life – in order that I may boast on the day of Christ that I did not run or labour for nothing. But even if I am being poured out like a drink offering on the sacrifice and service coming from your faith, I am glad and rejoice with all of you. So you too should be glad and rejoice with me.

Journeys can often be smooth and uneventful, but there are many times when they are anything but. I guess you've all got your stories of journeys where things went wrong. As we remember the theme of this week, the fiftieth anniversary of the ascent of Mount Everest back in 1953, perhaps it's just worth a reflection on the pitfalls and hazards that went into that ascent; the crevasses and ice walls. . . Just three days before Hillary and Tensing actually got to the summit, there was another attempt. Two men, Bourdillon and Evans didn't make it. Their oxygen supply went wrong and suddenly they were surrounded by weather closing in on them and they never made it to the top. They had to turn back down, giving the opportunity for Hillary and Tensing to get there first.

There are all sorts of pitfalls and hazards on any journey. As we go to the Scriptures we see that that is exactly the same with the journey of God's people. In the Old Testament, looking at God's people travelling from Egypt through to the Promised Land, we see all sorts of pitfalls and hazards. And it's the same as we come to the people of God in New Testament days. Often we see the same theme being used of God's people as the pilgrim people of God, heading towards the Promised Land. But again, it's not a straightforward journey. There are many pitfalls and hazards as we travel together to the Promised Land – glory itself. As we look at the importance of this journey that we are already on, it's important for us to be realistic about the difficulties that we face, but also that we can gain biblical wisdom on how we might surmount them. We're going to look at the church in Philippi as a case study. What pitfalls could Paul see that they were facing and how did he advise them to resolve those issues?

Hazards on the journey

Disunity

Paul is, on the whole, very pleased with the church in Philippi. But there were some things that were not quite right. There was disunity within God's people, verses 1 and 2: 'If you have any encouragement from being united with Christ . . . any comfort . . . any tenderness . . .' verse 2 'then make my joy complete by being like-minded, having the same love, being one in spirit and purpose.' Often with Paul's letters it's a bit like looking at a photographic negative. If you've got the negative you can work out what the picture looks like. If you've got the text, you can find out what the church in Philippi was like. Verse 2, clearly there were people who were not like-minded there, who did not have the same love. There were people who were not one in spirit. There was disunity within the body of Christ in Philippi. We see it not just in verses 1 and 2, but we also see it elsewhere. So for example, you might want to turn to chapter 4 and verse 2 where we read these words, 'I plead with you Euodia and I plead with Syntyche (two women within the church in Philippi) to agree with each other in the Lord.' We don't know whether it was a doctrinal issue that they were struggling with, but there was a dispute and disunity within the church. We see it also hinted at back in 1:7,8. Paul says, 'It is right for me to feel this way about all of you, since I have you in my heart; for whether I am in chains or defending or confirming the gospel, *all* of you are sharing God's grace. God can testify how I long for *all* of you with the affection of Christ Jesus.'

Go back to what we were witnessing back in February and March in the United Nations and we saw profound disunity within the Security Council when nations, for whatever reason, could not agree together. We say that's the United Nations, it's not the church. But there can be profound disunity within the local church, like Philippi; within a Christian organisation. Verses 3 and 4 of chapter 2, 'Do nothing out of selfish ambition or vain conceit, but in humility consider others better than yourselves.' There was this pride, this competitive spirit, perhaps within the leadership, as they pitted themselves against one another, with one person wanting to make a name for themselves and for their ministry, and others wanting to make a name for themselves. We see it also in Paul's own experience. He has been on the receiving end, and surely that is why he includes this little section back in chapter 1, verses 15-18: 'It is true that some preach Christ out of envy and rivalry . . . The former preach Christ out of selfish ambition, not sincerely, supposing that they can stir up trouble for me while I am in chains.' Again that's something that we see whenever we have a leadership election for a political party; people wanting to make a name for themselves. We see them arguing like anything as they seek to gain control. But it's also within the church – rivalry, wanting to make a name for yourself and for *your* ministry over against others. It was there in Philippi.

Don't complain

Chapter 2 verse 14: 'Do everything without complaining or arguing.' Why else would Paul say that unless there was actually moaning going on? The commentaries say that the word which Paul uses here is the word that is used in the Greek text of the Old Testament, all through the book of Numbers, to describe what the Israelites did as they grumbled through the desert. 'We haven't got any water, we haven't got any food.' All those sorts of things. 'We don't like the music, we don't like that preacher, we don't like the new pastor.' There was complaining going on behind the scenes.

Now we say to ourselves, it would be better if those things weren't there, but it's not particularly serious. It's not like the situation in

Galatia where Paul had to write the letter because there was doctrinal error going on; people adopting another gospel that was no gospel at all. Surely it's not like the situation in Colossae, where Paul had to write because again there was doctrinal heresy. He had to root that out in Galatia and Colossae, but this is different, isn't it, in Philippi? But we're wrong! Paul had to write to these folk, because it is *dreadfully* serious when things like disunity, rivalry and complaining start to take over in a local church, or in a Christian organisation. Just reflect for a moment, perhaps on past experience, perhaps even very painful current experiences where there is disunity or that background of complaining. Could it be that that is part of the reason why it is difficult to see progress in the gospel? Is that part of the reason why your leaders find themselves paralysed? These things that we might want to sweep under the carpet – 'it's just a little local problem' – Paul recognised were serious enough for him to write a letter. Here are some of the pitfalls and the hazards in discipleship, momentous things that can paralyse the progress of a church. Are we part of that group that are moaning and grumbling? Are we part of that faction that is pitted against that other group within the church? It's so easy for us to slip into these things.

Overcoming the obstacles

How does Paul teach them to overcome these problems? We need to ask the question 'What is the path that the Lord Jesus took?' Let's look together at verses 9-11 and see where Jesus actually ended up. 'Therefore God exalted him to the highest place and gave him the name that is above every name, that at the name of Jesus every knee should bow, in heaven and on earth and under the earth, and every tongue confess that Jesus Christ is Lord, to the glory of God the Father.'

He's ended up on the summit. But how did he get there? In your mind's eye, transport yourselves to the top of Blencathra or Grisedale Pike. You're on one of those very high mountains in the northern fells. But you actually want to get to the highest of our northern fells here,

Skiddaw. In order to get to that highest point, there's only one way; you have to go down into the valley, in order to ascend to the summit. That is exactly the path that we see our Lord Jesus Christ taking in these verses. We see Jesus plunging downwards from the heights of verse 6. He is in the very nature God, and yet we see himself making himself nothing, verse 7. He's going downhill, he's taking the very nature of a servant. He is being made in human likeness and being found in appearance as a man, he is humbling himself. It's downhill from the heights of the Godhead. And he appears as an obedient servant who suffers. A suffering servant, who goes all the way to death on a cross. As we look at the journey that the Lord Jesus Christ has taken to the summit, we see that it is a journey that has gone progressively downwards. It is being dominated, driven and shaped by the cross. As opposed to grasping something, he has let go, and he has gone downwards. He has let go of his rights. He has revealed himself as an obedient servant, concerned for the interests of others, even us, as he journeyed to the cross.

Cross-shaped lives

If you've been to the Alps and you've made a cable car journey, as you're on the way up, another cable car is on the way down. Paul is very graphically wanting to put these things together, because the Philippian church want to be on the way up. They're wanting to make a name for themselves. Paul is saying the Lord Jesus Christ was going downhill, giving up his rights, concerned not for himself but for the interests of others. And the path that Jesus took is to be our path. The obstacles have been highlighted in verses 1-3. We've seen Jesus' journey in verses 6-11, and verses 4 and 5 show us the connection. 'Each of you should look not only to your own interests but also to the interests of others. Your attitude should be the same as that of Christ Jesus'. We must travel the way of the cross. That is what Paul is wanting to teach these Philippians. It is to shape our lives. We are to be progressively more and more cross-shaped. Perhaps if you've been walking on the fells and you've seen the sheep, they've been marked by the shepherd. And we've been marked with the cross. We are to be shaped by the cross. That is the authentic mark to show that we belong to our Lord Jesus Christ.

I want to just give a few words of personal testimony, then we'll get back to the rest of Philippians chapter 2. I was converted when I went off to college, then I was invited to some of the Christian Union meetings. I decided to go along with my friend to the Sunday nights, where the gospel was preached. It was the opportunity for you to invite non-Christian friends to hear the cross being explained. I went along for a term, Sunday by Sunday. They were great nights. I thoroughly enjoyed feeding on the Scriptures and wanting to be converted all over again. But there came a time when I decided, I'm not going to go to Sunday nights any more, I'll go to Saturday nights. Saturday nights were when they had the Bible readings. They were for believers, and that seemed to be the appropriate thing to do, now that I had become a Christian. I would move from hearing about the cross, to study other things and grow as a Christian. I guess there were many good reasons for doing that, but in some ways it was actually a very profound mistake, because in some ways we never get beyond the cross. We are saved by the cross of our Lord Jesus Christ, because he stood in our place and took our sins.

We are saved by the cross, but also in our Christian discipleship, if it is to mean anything, we are to be those who are to be shaped by the cross. Now this dawned for me only in recent years, in a sort of crystal clarity. Because as I was teaching the Bible, quite often I would be in the epistles in the New Testament, and from time to time there would be a wonderful passage just like in Philippians 2 where Paul gets carried away and starts telling us the gospel all over again. But he's doing it for Christians, because the epistles are written to churches. So I started to think, why is it that Paul is preaching the gospel to Christians? They don't need it. It's non-Christians who need the gospel. I'd look at one or two commentaries and they would say, Paul is so thrilled with the gospel, he just sort of slips it in every now and again.

That's not right. Paul always puts things in for a purpose. So for example, come with me to Titus 3:2. Paul says that you are to teach the people to show true humility towards all people. The problem was that some Christians were feeling rather superior to the non-Christians around them. They were thinking, we're far better than them, because these Cretan non-Christians lie. How is Paul going to teach them to show proper humility? He preaches the cross! But he is preaching the cross to believers. He says, verse 3, 'At one time we too were foolish, disobedient, deceived and enslaved by all kind of passions and pleasures. We lived in malice and envy . . . But when the kindness and love of God our Saviour appeared, he saved us'. And he goes on in this wonderful section about the gospel, about what the cross has achieved. But notice, he is preaching the gospel to Christians, in order to teach Christians how to be humble and to live alongside non-Christians around them. To help them to see that we are no better, we are simply forgiven, he goes back to the cross.

Peter also does it. In 1 Peter 2:24 we read these words, 'Jesus himself bore our sins in his body on the tree so that we might die to sins and live for righteousness'. There is no clearer statement about the fact that we are saved through the cross of our Lord Jesus Christ. But why did Peter include it here? Why is he telling Christians this? Because he is struggling with the issue 'How can I get people who are employees to serve faithfully in the workplace?' Peter says, 'I'll preach the cross.' Time and time again as we look through the epistles, the resolution of the issues is by seeing the cross portrayed again.

That is what Paul wants to see. The cross saves us, and the cross must shape our lives. Therefore, Paul and Peter and all the folk who were involved in writing the New Testament were convinced that we must never graduate from the cross. The cross is to save us and we go back to the cross, day by day, as we remind ourselves that we are forgiven people because of what the Lord Jesus Christ accomplished there. But also, the cross is to shape us and the way we live for Christ in our day. Now this is a vital thing that Paul wants to drum home.

What does this route look like?

Let's now return to Philippians and we come to verse 12. Paul says, 'work out your salvation'. Work it out for yourself. Not by any sense meaning 'you've got to save yourself.' The cross saves us. But he is say-ing work out for yourself in your situation your own way forward to the summit. You've seen how Christ did it, now let's work it out. Yes we will do it with fear and trembling because it is not an easy task to embrace the journey to the cross, the journey of service, the journey of suffering. But it is a route that we will take with God's help because it is God who is at work in you, verse 13, to will and to act accord-ing to his good purpose.

You might get a mathematics puzzle and you have to work it out. I have a daughter who is fourteen and from time to time it's 'Can you help me with my homework?' The problem is that as you look at the maths, it's done in completely different ways from when you or I were at school. You think 'this is the way I do it' and Rachel will say 'that's not the way we've been taught at school.' You think, help! I don't think I can do this. And you turn over the page and then you see a worked example. You think, I'll do the worked example and that will help me to know the way forward. Paul, in the rest of Philippians chapter 2, gives three worked examples of what it will mean for you and I to work out our own salvation, go the way of the cross and adopt a cross-shaped life.

Paul

So come with me to verses 17 and 18. 'Even if I am being poured out like a drink offering on the sacrifice and service coming from your faith, I am glad . . . ' As we look at Paul, we see somebody who is pouring out his life. It's like a bottle; what happens when you start pouring out the contents? It empties itself until eventually there is nothing left. Our minds go back to what we have been told about the Lord Jesus Christ in Philippians 2, 'He made himself nothing.' He poured himself out. Paul is an example of somebody who is living a cross-shaped life. Tell Paul that he can move on from the cross and he would say 'Never! I never graduate from the cross.'

Timothy

Let's look at verses 20-21: 'I have no-one else like him who takes a genuine interest in your welfare. For everyone looks out for his own interests, not those of Jesus Christ.' Timothy is different. He's not concerned for his own interests, he's concerned for the interests of Christ, the interests of those around him. Sounds a bit like the Lord Jesus Christ again, doesn't it? As we go back to verse 4: 'Each of you should look not only to your own interests, but also to the interests of others. Your attitude should be the same as that of Christ Jesus'. Tell Timothy that he can move on from the cross? That he's been a Christian for quite a few years, he can move on from that, and he would say 'Never! The cross is shaping my life day by day as I look for the interests of others.'

Epaphroditus

What do we know about Epaphroditus? There is one key feature that is spelled out about Epaphroditus. Verse 29, 'Welcome him . . . with great joy, and honour men like him, because he almost died for the work of Christ, risking his life to make up for the help you could not give me.' Epaphroditus is somebody else who has been stamped with the cross, saved by the cross, but then he is shaped by the cross for which he is prepared to risk his life in the service of others. It sounds a bit like the Lord Jesus Christ, doesn't it? Humbling himself and going all the way to the cross. Giving up his life for us. Tell Epaphroditus, 'You've been a Christian for quite a few years now, you're really useful in the Lord's service, you're wonderful. But you can move on from the cross.' Epaphroditus would say, 'We never graduate from the cross. It is to shape the whole of my life and my direction.'

All these are worked examples of humility, service, suffering and sacrifice, each shaped by the cross of our Lord Jesus Christ. They don't just believe the cross, but they are living it out in the way in which they are operating. As we now seek to work out what that means in our situation, we will need to translate it into our twenty-first century context. But as we become more and more shaped by the cross, we become more and more different, lights in the darkness that Paul refers to in verses 15-16, so that we can make a difference in our generation. Because people will see that the message of the cross is married to a life shaped by the cross, and as these two things come together, there we have the authentic message and ministry that Paul is longing for.

He doesn't just want preachers of the cross, but he wants those shaped by the cross. So that people cannot just hear it, but see it, and so magnify the cross of our Lord Jesus Christ.

I wonder what a cross-shaped life will look like for you and me? In the workplace? A life poured out for others, where we look for the interests of others, where we're prepared to suffer for others. What will a cross-shaped life look like within your local fellowship, or your Christian organisation? A life where you pour yourself out for others rather than making a name for yourself? A place where you are looking for the interests of others, rather than your own interests first and your wants and your desires and all the rest of it? What will a cross-shaped life look for you?

Work it out with God's help. But as you embrace a cross-shaped life, surely there will be no surprise if we find the murmurings start to die down, the rivalries start to dissipate. Surely we will find that there is such a tremendous unity in the local church, that we can go forward in gospel progress. This is biblical, cross-shaped, cross-focused, New Testament thinking. It's not just that Paul can see a problem and say, sort yourselves out! He portrays the cross of our Lord Jesus Christ and says that is the way. And we all stumble and fail but he says, God is at work in you, he will help you by the Spirit of our crucified Lord Jesus Christ, he will lead you in ways that will please him to make that cross-shaped life a reality in your own life and fellowship. The one thing that you cannot forget in your Christian journey is the cross of our Lord Jesus Christ. You cannot leave it behind, you must take it with you and be shaped by it.

One final thing. Sir Edmund Hillary and Tensing Norgay emerged on the summit of Mount Everest, 11.30 am, the 29th of May 1953. They spent fifteen minutes on the summit. They did various things, they took pictures of each other. But there was one final thing that Hillary did before he went down. He dug a little hole in the ice and put something that the expedition leader John Hunt had given him and which he had put in his pocket. It was a cross. As I was thinking that, it occurred to me, that all the way up that long ascent through all the pitfalls, through all the difficulties that Hillary and Tensing went through, throughout all the problems of the weather and whether it would clear in time, and all those sorts of things, Hillary was carrying a cross. All the way to the summit. Perhaps that's just a little picture that we can go away with. All the way in our Christian pilgrimage, wherever we are, despite all the things that are thrown against us, all the way to the summit, we will need to be those who take up that cross daily and follow him. A life saved by the cross, of course, but also a life shaped by the cross.

The Pitfalls and Hazards in Discipleship II

by Peter Maiden

PETER MAIDEN

Keswick's current chairman and International Director of Operation Mobilisation, Peter is a very busy man. He travels extensively to fulfil his commitments with OM – overseeing the day-to-day co-ordination of its ministry in eighty-two countries worldwide. Peter is also an Elder at Hebron Evangelical church in Carlisle where he lives and manages to include itinerant Bible teaching in the UK and overseas in his schedule. Peter enjoys family life with his wife Win and their three children and grandchild, as well as endurance sports. In particular he loves long distance running, fell walking and long distance cycling.

The Pitfalls and Hazards of Discipleship

Introduction

We're going to look at 1 Samuel chapter 13 and commence to read at verse 5. Jonathan has just destroyed a Philistine garrison and Saul is pretty convinced that this means trouble for Israel. We'll pick up the story in verse 5 and I'm going to read from the New Living Translation.

The Philistines mustered a mighty army of three thousand chariots, six thousand horsemen and as many warriors as the grains of sand along the seashore. They camped at Michmash, east of Beth Aven. When the men of Israel saw the vast number of enemy troops they lost their nerve entirely and tried to hide in caves, holes, rocks, tombs and cisterns. Some of them crossed the river Jordan and escaped into the land of Gad and Gilead. Meanwhile Saul stayed at Gilgal and his men were trembling with fear. Saul waited there seven days for Samuel, as Samuel had instructed him earlier. But Samuel still didn't come. Saul realised that his troops were rapidly slipping away, so he demanded, 'Bring *me* the burnt offering and the peace offerings,' and Saul sacrificed the burnt offering himself.

Just as Saul was finishing with the burnt offering, Samuel arrived. Saul went out to meet and welcome him. But Samuel said, 'What is this you have done?' Saul replied, 'I saw my men scattering from me, and you didn't arrive when you said you would, and the Philistines are at Michmash, ready for battle. So, I said, the Philistines are ready to march against us and I haven't even asked for the Lord's help. So I felt obliged to offer the burnt offering myself before you came.

'How foolish!', Samuel exclaimed. 'You've disobeyed the command of the Lord your God. Had you obeyed the Lord he would have established your kingdom over Israel forever. But now, your dynasty must end. For the Lord has sought out a man after his own heart. The Lord has already chosen him to be king over his people, for you have not obeyed the Lord's command.'

I wonder how many of you in the tent this evening have climbed Latrigg. That's the little bump just in front of Skiddaw. Climbed is a bit of an exaggeration really, isn't it? It's a sort of afternoon amble up the mountain path. But let me tell you of two incidents that I've had on Latrigg. Two years ago I was on my way up Latrigg and I saw a man lying at the side of the path. He had been coming down and he'd slipped on his way down, gone over and broken his leg. Fortunately I had my mobile phone with me and I rang the mountain rescue and got him safely down.

Last year I was going up the same little hill and one of our own volunteers working at the Convention had fallen and broken her wrist, just on the mild slopes of Latrigg. The simplest mountains, the simplest hills contain unexpected hazards. And our subject this week is from base camp to summit. I wonder how many who worshipped with us at Keswick last year are no longer following Christ? They began their journey, but they've fallen. And they haven't got up again – they've stayed down. So many it seems in our country these days are either spiritually stillborn or there are many spiritual infant deaths taking place. Pause for a moment and think of people you might know who walked with Christ and no longer are doing so.

It seems that no group of people are immune from this. In the world of missions I regularly come across people who once walked with Christ, seemed to serve him faithfully, often sacrificially. But something, somewhere went wrong. Today they are nowhere spiritually. Others, to put it bluntly, seem to get stuck; saved, but stuck. They seem to settle down spiritually. On the surface things appear OK, church attendance continues. No grave signs of public sin, but also no great signs of spiritual development. I hope we can discover some of the reasons for the many cases of stunted growth that we see in the Christian church. I want to do this by concentrating our thinking around one man, who had every reason to be a real champion for God. But his life ended in spiritual disgrace.

Saul – God's anointed leader

Let's pick up the story in chapter nine of 1 Samuel. Verse one shows us that Saul was born into privilege. Kish his father is described as a rich influential man, from the tribe of Benjamin. Saul was born into a family of influence. He also had exceptional physical attributes. He was the most handsome man in Israel, head and shoulders taller than anyone else in the land. But it wasn't just that nature had smiled on Saul. Saul was God's anointed man. Along with his servant, Saul goes looking for Samuel and as Samuel comes towards him, God says to Samuel (9:17), 'That's the man!' Saul's the man I told you about. He will rule over my people. So, chapter 10:1, Samuel takes a flask of olive oil and pours it over Saul's head. As he does so, he says 'I am doing this because the Lord has appointed you to be ruler over his people.'

How is this young man going to receive all this? How is he going to respond to it? Initially he shows that essential quality of humility. As Samuel speaks of God's anointing, Saul replies, 'I am only from Benjamin, the smallest tribe in the land. My family is the least important of all the families of the tribe. Why are you talking to me like this?' A beautiful, humble response from this young man. But the choice, the anointing of God is quickly confirmed by clear evidence of the power of God's Spirit at work in this young man's life. On his way home from meeting Samuel, Samuel informs him that when he arrives at Gibeah he'll meet a band of prophets coming down from the altar on the hill. And at that time Samuel said to him (10:6): 'The Spirit of the Lord will come upon you, Saul, with power, and you will prophesy with those prophets. You will be changed into a different person.' And it's exactly as it turned out to be. Verse 9 in the same chapter: Saul turned to leave and God changed his heart and all of Samuel's signs were fulfilled that day.

Things happened extraordinarily quickly for Saul. He's anointed king of Israel. Within a matter of weeks he has to raise an army. And as he does so, I think you see some of the qualities of a leader who knows the anointing of the Spirit of God. Just turn the page to chapter 11:6. 'The Spirit of God came mightily upon Saul and he became angry' – righteous anger, I believe. He takes two oxen, cuts the oxen in pieces and sends the messengers to carry them throughout Israel with this message: 'This is what's going to happen to the oxen of anyone who refuses to follow Saul and Samuel into battle.'

This is decisive leadership if ever you wanted to see it, from this young, humble, anointed man of God. It's no wonder that three hundred thousand men of Israel and thirty thousand men of Judah were mobilised that day. Now often people who become strong, decisive leaders become very insensitive. They tend to lack restraint, sometimes compassion. But that's not immediately evident in this young man. Saul takes the army out and they have great victory.

Back at his anointing as king, not everyone was happy. Some complained – how can this man save us? They despised him, they refused to bring him gifts. Saul's companions want to seize the moment. The moment of great victory, Saul, should be your opportunity for revenge (11:12). A real opportunity for Saul to get even. Saul replies, 'No one will be executed today. Today the Lord has rescued Israel.' Here you have strength and mercy in wonderful combination. Looks like a really great story unfolding, doesn't it? Surely this man is going to take his place in chapters such as Hebrews 11, which describes the people of faith in Israel whom God uses so dramatically. But when you get to that chapter, you find an obvious silence about Saul. Samuel is there, David the second king of the land, but silence when it comes to Saul.

Saul – the failure

If we go forward to the end of Saul's life we'll see the reason for the silence. Let's look at chapter 31 of 1 Samuel. Israel is being attacked by the Philistines. Remember these are the armies that Saul has a divine commission to deliver Israel from. Saul is wounded by Philistine archers and eventually has to fall on his own sword. I'm sure he could only begin to imagine what the Philistines would have done to him if they'd found him alive. So the king, with a divine commission to deliver Israel from the Philistines, is tragically dying at their hands. Such is the measure of this man's failure. But it actually gets worse. The next day when the Philistines went out to strip the dead, they found the bodies of Saul and his three sons on Mount Gilboa. They cut off Saul's head, stripped off his armour, proclaimed the news of his death in the pagan temple and to the people throughout the land. They placed his armour in the temple of the Ashtoreths and fastened his body to the wall of the city of Beth Shan.

Now just go back into your mind to the defeat of Goliath. Remember when he was defeated his sword was taken into Israel's sanctuary and it became a trophy. What a reversal as Saul's head and armour becomes a source of rejoicing in pagan temples and pagan cities, bringing the God of Israel public distress. Because it can, and it does, still happen. People who start the mountain well fall dramatically, and sometimes publicly, and bring the glory of God into disgrace. What a tragic end after such a promising beginning.

Neglecting spiritual disciplines

So where did it all go wrong for Saul? Where does it go wrong so often for me, and possibly for you? What I want to say is that discipleship is not rocket science. Sometimes we do make the Christian life and Christian living very complex. So often it goes wrong for us, or certainly for me, when I neglect basic spiritual disciplines.

Saul's impatience was part of his downfall. Look forward to chapter 13. It's the first moment of crisis in the leadership of king

Saul. So far things have really gone very well for him. But now the Philistine army is arrayed against him and it's massive. It's described as 'as many warriors as the grains of sand along the seashore,' and the sight of the army is enough to send the men of Israel scurrying into any cover they can find. Pick up the story in the middle of verse 7, 1 Samuel 13:7. 'Meanwhile Saul stayed at Gilgal and his men were trembling with fear. Saul waited there seven days for Samuel as Samuel had instructed him earlier, but Samuel didn't come. Saul realised that his troops were rapidly slipping away.'

Being self-sufficient

This is a significant crisis for this young leader. No doubt he feels he must make a move or the whole army will desert. So (v9) he demands, 'Bring me the burnt offering and the peace offerings.' Saul sacrifices the burnt offerings himself. Commentators struggle to define the actual sin of which Saul is guilty here. But there's disobedience at the heart of it. 'How foolish', Samuel exclaims, 'you've disobeyed the command of the Lord your God.' The consequences for Saul are extremely severe (v13). Your dynasty must end, Samuel says, (v14). And there's a separation (v15), between Samuel and Saul. Never again will they enjoy the same relationship. What's happening here? By sacrificing is Saul attempting to extend his powers to include a priestly role as well as a military one? Has he lost confidence in God? Is he failing to rely on God? Verse 12 is interesting. He says to Samuel, 'I haven't even asked for the Lord's help, so I felt obliged to offer the burnt offerings myself.' Sounds like a last minute thought, doesn't it? I believe that what we have here is a man who is neglecting to listen to God. He's becoming a self-sufficient man.

No time for God

A quick look into the next chapter will give you another example. Due to the decisive daring of Jonathan, in stark contrast to the indecisive hesitancy of Saul, the Philistines are now in a panic (v15). Saul shouts to Ahijah, 'Bring the ephod here' (v18). Saul is still expecting explicit, divine orders in this situation. But while he's talking to the priest, the confusion amongst the Philistines increases and then you read these incredible words: 'We should be waiting for orders, but never mind. Too much is happening! Let's go, we haven't time to wait on God.'

I was talking to a very close friend recently. He's an Indian surgeon who's done a magnificent work in the slums of Bombay. Recently he commenced a ministry to those dying of HIV/AIDS in the slums. A small team came to work with him. At the start of the work, the team decided to spend two days a week in prayer. I was with my friend Stephen at the time and he said, 'I couldn't understand it. People are dying! Two days in prayer?! Half a day I can understand, but two days a week?!' Fortunately my friend kept his mouth shut. Today he's very glad that he did. His conviction is that more is being accomplished in those four working days than ever he could have imagined in the six working days. I said, 'that's great Stephen, but just one correction, I think they are working six days, because prayer is some of the most precious work we can ever involve ourselves in.' Christian discipleship, my brothers and sisters, is not rocket science. Saul's tragic failure begins as self-sufficiency grows within his heart. He has no time to wait for God; no time to listen.

In our hectic, twenty-first century lifestyle, it surely is one of my greatest dangers, and possibly yours. We neglect the basic disciplines, we don't give time to listen for God. Another Asian friend of mine was travelling with me in the UK. We visited a number of churches. After a number of services he said, 'Peter, when does God get time to speak to you English?' I said, 'What do you mean?' He said, 'My impression of your services is that they are so rushed, and they're so organised that there's no time just to listen for God.' I trust that one result of my talk this evening might be that we'll build some changes into our schedules. We'll build time for God, time to listen to him, time to express our dependency upon him.

Simple obedience

This self-sufficiency, this neglect of his relationship with God led to a second problem. When I read the story of Saul's life I get very frustrated. I say, 'Saul, why don't you just listen and obey?!' I get frustrated until I think of my own life, and then I appreciate Saul a little more.

'Saul, why can't you just listen to God and obey him?! Why don't you just simply obey his every word?' But simple obedience didn't come easily to Saul. If I'm not listening to God, my relationship becomes distant, and then the confidence to trust and obey is gradually eroded. We've only got time for one example. There are many we could choose, but look at chapter 15. You can see (v2) that through Samuel, God tells Saul, 'I've decided to settle accounts with the nation of Amalek.' The Amalekites were nomadic people. They lived in the desert between the southern borders of Judah, Egypt and extended south into the Sinai Peninsula. We need to understand a bit about them to understand this passage. It seems very brutal to us. The Amalekites had tried to prevent Israel from reaching Sinai after they had crossed the Red Sea.

> Then the Lord instructed Moses, 'Write this down as a permanent record, and announce it to Joshua: I will blot out every trace of Amalek from under heaven.' Moses built an altar there and called it 'The Lord is My Banner.' He said, 'They have dared to raise their fist against the Lord's throne, so now the Lord will be at war with Amalek generation after generation' (Ex. 17:14).

We've got a nation which is raising its fist to the God of heaven. God is giving to Saul the responsibility to carry out his divine sentence against the Amalekites. This isn't a war of aggression. It's not a war of self-defence. This is a true, holy war. Saul is to carry out God's judgment on Amalek.

Now in our culture we may be very surprised by the severity of the commands which follow. God says, 'You must completely destroy the whole nation.' But this wouldn't seem strange to the ear of an Israelite. You see, the victory would be the Lord's over the Amalekites. It was *his* judgment that they were carrying out. There was to be no material advantage for the army or the nation. The command to Saul was clear. And the reasons would have been equally clear. Was this Saul's last opportunity to obey the Lord? Was this his opportunity to make up for all his recent failures? Saul moves against the Amalekites. He suddenly engages in a great slaughter, but it's not the total destruction which the judgment of God demanded. Look at verse 7, 'Saul slaughtered the Amalekites from Havilah all the way to Shur, east of Egypt, captured Agag the Amalekite king but completely destroyed everything else. Saul and his men spared Agag's life, kept the best of the sheep and the cattle, the fat calves, the lambs', everything that appealed to them. They destroy only what was worthless or of poor quality. Saul's only interest is his own interest. Don't you think, Saul, why will you not just simply obey?

Why do I find total obedience, total commitment such a struggle? Why do I still so often try and hold back areas of my life from divine control? What held Saul back? We can't be sure, but no doubt it was many of those things which hold me back. I wonder if his saving of the best of sheep and cattle made him something of a hero in front of his men. It must have been for their advantage. And why ever did he save king Agag? Was he expecting that he would negotiate some huge ransom for him? I know those are huge issues with me. So often we have the choice between acceptance by our friends or total obedience. In our materialistic, consumer-driven age, is this not still one of the most significant issues for us? Are we like Saul, going to hold back the best in our commitment? The tithe principle show that first, the best is his by right, not the leftovers. I talk to many people who say I just couldn't contemplate that. Some task they're being challenged to consider – I couldn't contemplate it. What do they mean? They mean 'I'm too busy to contemplate the task you're suggesting.' And what do they mean when they say, 'I'm too busy'? Sometimes, not all cases, what they mean is this: 'to maintain my chosen lifestyle I must live at a certain pace. I could live comfortably at a much lower lifestyle, but such a choice I will never consider.'

Learn to repent

Saul stopped listening to God. His relationship became distant. Trust, and then obedience, was eroded. But finally, let's look at possibly the most tragic aspect of his life. When he failed in the way I've just described, Saul never learned to repent. All you see in Saul is the attempt at self-justification. Saul has begun to sacrifice because Samuel hasn't arrived within the appointed period. You read in chapter 13:10

as Saul was finishing with the burnt offerings, Samuel arrived. He wasn't very late. Saul went out to welcome him. He greets Samuel as his brother sacrificer, as if he now thinks of himself as the complete priest. Then he seems to blame Samuel (v11), 'I saw my men scattering from me, and you didn't arrive when you said you would.'

If we look at the destruction of the Amalekites, again you find Samuel getting an interesting response from Saul. Chapter 15:13, Saul greeted Samuel cheerfully. 'May the Lord bless you,' he said, 'I've carried out the Lord's commands.' Saul knew there had been a divine command, and that he hadn't obeyed it. But again, it's very unlikely that if Saul's conscience hadn't charged him with disobedience, he would have been so enthusiastic in proclaiming his obedience. Saul is seeking to prevent Samuel from reproving him.

Just a little later a ray of hope seems to appear. Look at 15:24. Then Saul finally admitted, 'I've disobeyed your instructions and the Lord's commands.' Now that sounds much better, Saul. But he can't avoid those words of mitigation and justification. 'I was afraid of the people. I did what they demanded.' Compare David's repentance to Saul's, the moment Nathan showed David his sin. He repented with absolutely no attempt at self-justification. 'I've sinned against the Lord.' In Psalm 51, he justifies God rather than himself. 'I know my sins, they are ever before me. Against you, you only have I sinned and done what is evil in your sight, so that you are justified when you judge.'

Not my fault

So what does Saul do instead of repentance? He's constantly trying to pass the buck. Chapter 13, 'You didn't come within the appointed time'. Chapter 15, 'the army spared the best of the cattle.' Chapter 15 again, 'I was afraid of the people, I did what they demanded.' Passing the buck goes right back to the garden of Eden, but it's also a contemporary excuse. My church is not what it should be. In a Christian marriage, where partners are not going on for God, you'll often find one partner blaming the other. Some modern counselling methods appear to make blame-shifting legitimate. It's never finally our responsibility. Saul had immense pressures in his life, incredibly difficult issues to deal with. But he never appeared to take final responsibility for his failure. And even with all the complexities of his life, the final respon-sibility was his.

God seeks obedience

Secondly, note, how he not only seeks to justify himself, but he actually tries to spiritualise his failures. Look at one final verse, 15:15. It's true, he says, the army spared the best of the sheep and cattle, but they're going to sacrifice them to the Lord your God. I wonder how significant it is that Saul doesn't refer to the Lord *our* God, but the Lord *your* God. He's saying, 'Samuel, eventually they're going to be sacrificed. Ultimately the Lord's command of complete destruction will be fulfilled.' In response to that pathetic attempt at self-justification, Samuel teaches a vital lesson for us all. It's there in verse 22. Samuel replied, 'What is more pleasing to the Lord? Your burnt offerings, sacrifices, or your obedience to his voice? Obedience is far better than sacrifice; listening to him much better than the offering of the fat of rams.' You can't cover your disobedi-ence by ceremonial acts of public worship.

I wonder if we do that? We know that not all is not well with us in our walk with God, our obedience far from complete. But we continue to attend public worship and often go away from public worship feeling so much better, that we're doing what the Lord expects. But the Lord says to us, my only expectation is obedience. I was at a church not so long ago where things seemed to be really heavy, and after a communion service I asked the elder why things were such a struggle. He described two families in that church who'd been at loggerheads for (I think) more than twenty years. And they hadn't spoken to each other. Yet Sunday by Sunday they were coming to the communion rail together and no doubt going away feeling so much better, that they were obeying the Lord by going through this public act of worship. I think God would say to them what he said to Saul: obedience is what I'm looking for.

What a tragic story. And it's not the only one like it in Scripture. A speaker last week suggested that two-thirds of those who started well in their walk with God, recorded in Scripture, don't finish well. I do know that a large number of people, who start well in Scripture in their walk with God, do not finish well. In a congregation of this size there must be some who are not doing well spiritually, right now. We haven't been waiting, we haven't been listening. Trust has eroded, and along with that, obedience. Sad but, praise God, not fatal.

How glad we are that we worship the God of the second opportunity. Many of us testify, and I would certainly be one of them, not just the second, but countless opportunities. It doesn't have to end where Saul ended. We just have to look at Saul's contemporary, David, to be assured of that. He fell spectacularly. In some ways you might say his fall was far greater than Saul's. But his repentance, his determination to once again live in obedience to God was equally spectacular and truly moving.

Look how far you have fallen

If you know that you are in a Saul-like state, remember with me what the Lord Jesus said to the Ephesian church in Revelation 2. They weren't loving Jesus as they had previously. Jesus said three simple things to them: he said look how far you've fallen from your first love. Remember it. Some of us can remember better days in our walk with God. Jesus says it's good to remember such days.

Turn back to me

Second instruction: turn back to me, in sorrow and joy at his mercy and his willingness to help us to renew our commitment. I have to do that time and time again. One of the verses of Scripture which has been a deep encouragement to me is Paul's words to the Corinthians. I love the Living Bible paraphrase: 'I'm often knocked down but I'm not knocked out.' That's my testimony: often knocked down, often on my nose in the dust spiritually, but by the grace of God and *only* by the grace of God, not knocked out.

If you're down, if you're Saul-like in your spiritual state tonight, don't stay down! I used to be a rock climber in a very amateurish sort of way. I used to climb Shepherd's Crag, just along the Borrowdale Valley there. And I'll never forget the day I fell. I was climbing second, so I was OK, but the guy above me wasn't very good and he let me go a long way. I remember the cracking nylon rope as I went back and forward and looked at the lake below me. I was helped down eventually and I've never climbed since. That's all right, I think, physically. But if you find yourself down spiritually; you're climbing and you drop, don't stay down! Get back on the road. Get back on the rock. Look how far you've fallen. 'Turn back to me again.'

Do what you did at first

Remember those days of closer walk. I'm sure basic disciplines were important to you. You had a hunger for the word. You spent time in his presence. You loved to be with your brothers and sisters in Christ, growing together. You took time to tell others about your love for Christ. If you're Saul-like in your spiritual condition this evening, remember better days. Turn back to God and start doing again those things that you were doing when you had better spiritual times. Tonight the challenge is 'Come back home', into intimate relationship with a Father who waits, longingly, to receive you.

A Grace Response to Muslims
by Steve Bell

STEVE BELL

Converted in his mid-teens through various influences – Anglican, street preaching and an AOG youth Bible group – Steve eventually became a youth leader in his late teens and was encouraged in seeing the group grow from a handful to over sixty people. Originally a commercial artist, he later trained as an English teacher and worked in multicultural inner-city schools before going to the Middle East for ten years as a tentmaking mission worker. After being asked to leave by the secret police, he returned to the UK as Director of Carey College, then Action Partners ministries. In 2002, Steve set up 'Friendship First', a resource service helping 'ordinary' Christians relate the good news about Jesus to 'ordinary' Muslims. He is married to Julia and loves walking, classical music and collecting postcards.

A Grace Response to Muslims

My prayer this morning is that I will not bear false witness against our neighbours, but that I will speak the truth in love. My prayer is that this lecture will not just be about information, but also impartation. My role with Friendship First is very much about attitude change, and I trust this morning there will be some of that.

If a grace response to Muslims is going to be possible, can we get hold of the idea that it is not some huge divine error that there are approximately 1.8 million Muslims resident in the UK, they're here in the purposes of God? I want to suggest that the challenge of Islam to evangelical Christians is not so much whether Britain will become an Islamic state by stealth, so much as questions like: 'Does our spiritual calibre exceed the Pharisaical righteousness which Islam requires of the Muslim?' 'How can we build genuine bridges of witness and relationship with ordinary Muslims without being naïve or complacent about the darker realities behind politicised Islam?' It's questions like this that have driven my preparation. And I want to look at, if we have time, eight cameos.

The roots of Mohammed

In the first one, we go to the roots of the prophet of Islam himself. We're going to look at something of the ethnic and theological

kinship between the Jewish and the Arab peoples. It takes us to
Genesis 16 where we see a very human situation in the household of
Abram, later named Abraham, and Sarai his wife, later re-named Sarah.
In Genesis 16:1 it says, 'Sarai, Abram's wife, was childless.' Trust me
when I say this is a catastrophe in Middle Eastern culture. Even
Orthodox Christian people today would consider divorce where
infertility is there, or the inability to bear sons. Now we westerners say,
what if it's the man's fault? I'm just reporting to you a cultural norm
at this point. So Sarai couldn't bear children. Will the solution to the
problem be by self-help (works), or will it be by divine assistance
(grace)? Verse 2 tells us that Sarai and Abram chose the self-help route.
She gave her maid Hagar, an Egyptian, to Abram as a surrogate mother. So self-help is somehow within the very DNA at this embryonic
stage both in the Judaistic and Islamic traditions. We're going to see
that as we go. Verse 4 tells us that when Hagar became pregnant with
Ishmael, she began to despise Sarai. This rivalry theme began within
the household. Verse 5: Sarai blames Abram. 'It's all your fault,' she says.
Verse 6, Sarai mistreats Hagar until Hagar, and this is significant, runs
away. She leaves the household.

In verse 7, Hagar is out in the desert and the angel of the Lord finds
Hagar beside a desert spring. I am delighted to be able to say today
that God is finding Muslims and producing for them springs of living
water in dry places. It was in the divine economy that Hagar should
survive and that the child within her, Ishmael, should survive. We go
to verse 8a. The angel asks Hagar the question, 'where have you come
from, and where are you going?' The key issue. Hagar was pregnant
with Ishmael who was a predecessor of the Arab race, and therefore a
forefather of Mohammed el-Qureshi, the founder of Islam who was
an Arab. He would carry a Saudi passport today. If you will understand
my reasoning here, it's as if the angel is saying, 'Hagar where have you
come from?' 'Ishmael where have you come from?' 'Mohammed
where have you come from?' 'Islam, where have you come from and
where are you going?'

There are not many politicians today who would not love the
answer to that question concerning Islam. Most Christians too are
interested in where Islam has come from. What are its real origins?

Many media people would like to know the answer to 'where Islam is going?' But it almost goes without saying that the destiny of Islam is most likely linked to its origin. And its origin is squarely within the household of Abraham. But we are not journalists or politicians. We are Bible-believing Christians who can say on the authority of the Scriptures, we believe that God is steering human history to his appointed end – Islam included. There cannot be any item or issue in contemporary society and world affairs which is beyond the sovereignty of God – Islam included. I find Bible-believing Christians often struggle here. And it's difficult to hold fear in our hearts and to firmly hang onto the sovereignty of God in world affairs. The two seem incompatible, but many of us as Christians try to do it. Why did God allow Islam to start and to flourish in the first place? We cannot hold to the sovereignty of God and fear that Islam is some sort of divine mistake.

Moving on to verse 8b. Hagar answers the first part of the question. She says, 'I'm running away from my mistress.' I find Bishop Kenneth Cragg so helpful here. I've summarised his book *The Call of the Minaret* in one quote. Here it is: 'The call of the minaret must always be for the Christian a call to retrieval. The objective is not as the Crusaders believed, the repossession of what Christendom once lost, but the restoration to Muslims of the Christ whom they have always missed.' 'Come back. Islam, come back. Sons of Ishmael, come back to the household.' That's the issue.

In verse 9, the angel calls Hagar to return. Come back to the house and submit. Interesting. You can't build a theology on this, but I find it so neat that the angel uses that word, submit. In Arabic, *tislem*. *Tislem* is the imperative in the Arabic for submit. 'Islam' means submission. A 'Muslim' is somebody who submits to God. The angel in effect is saying to Hagar return and do your 'islam' within the house. There's nothing wrong with the concept of Islamic submission to God, it's where you do your 'islam.' I hope that every one of you are submitted to God, through Jesus Christ.

Genesis 21:10: Hagar returns to the household. Ishmael is born. The friction starts all over again. Hagar is driven out of the house for good, and she's followed by the words of Sarah who says, 'Cast out the bondwoman and her son.' It's the very text which some of the Crusaders attacked Jerusalem with in the Middle Ages quoting this passage, to rid Jerusalem of Arabs. Again in 21:20, 'God preserved the life of Hagar and Ishmael in the wilderness.' It says God helped Hagar to see a well of water in dry places. Verse 20 says God was with Ishmael and he lived in the desert. Islam has always traditionally been a religion of the desert. It flourishes amongst Bedouin and pastoral, mobile communities more than in the western world. And God promised Abraham to make a nation of Ishmael. Notice it in Genesis 21:13, God says 'because he is your son.' In Genesis 17:20, God promises 'as for Ishmael ...' By the way, most names in the Middle East carry a meaning. Ishma El, or Ishmael, means 'Isma' – hears, 'el' – God. God hears. He says, 'as for Ishmael, I have heard you'. It's a play on the word. Semites love it. God says to him, 'I will bless him also.' Abraham has said to God, 'Oh, that Ishmael might live before you. You keep telling me about a promise of a son.' God is saying, 'I have spoken to you, you're going to have a son.' Isaac was the result. But he's saying, 'as for Ishmael, I have heard you and I'll bless him also, as you ask. I will make him fruitful and multiply him.'

Today there are over two hundred million sons of Ishmael, Arabs. And it says he will be father of twelve princes. A prince is an emir. An emir runs an emirate. Have you got the link? The Gulf is peopled by emirates. I find it interesting that there is a parallel that Jacob had twelve sons and Ishmael had twelve sons. Moving on to Genesis 25:18: the descendants of Ishmael settled in northern Arabia, today called Saudi Arabia. Ishmael's descendants scattered across the country 'from Havilah to Shur which is east of Egypt.' The clans descended from Ishmael camped as Bedouin close to one another.

We move on to an illustration of the family tree of Ishmael and Isaac. Isaac's sons produced prophets – Moses, David, Jesus. They produced scripture – Tawrat or Torah, the Zaboor or Psalms, the Injil or Gospel. While on Ishmael's line – nothing!. . . until five hundred and seventy years after the prophet, Jesus. (Speaking from the Muslim perspective there.) Five hundred and seventy years after the prophet Jesus, Mohammed el-Qureshi was born in Arabia. Now the sons of Ishmael could lift their heads up and say 'We have a prophet, we have scriptures.' Remember the tension theme at work between the two sides. Ishmael is the elder brother, Isaac the younger brother, and many of the works/grace tensions, which are found in the parable of the prodigal son, work their way out in the relationship of these two boys, and the negative attitude of the one line to the grace given to the other line.

A little testimony. . .

I've received recently the news that the fastest selling translation of the Bible today is the Arabic version of the Bible. The most popular version of the *Jesus* film today is in the Arabic language. The most visited Christian website is the Bible online in the Arabic language. Praise God for that.

The nature of Islam

Abraham is father of faith to Jew, to Christian and to Muslim. Friends, this is a *huge* open door! The next manual that we're producing, under Friendship First, is going to be to assist Christian school teachers for assemblies and RE, youth workers and children's workers. Men like Abraham provide huge open doors of witness to Muslim people. He is the Father of Faith. Jews relate to Abraham through Isaac's bloodline. Muslims relate to Abraham through Ishmael's bloodline: Abraham being the first Muslim in many Muslims' eyes. The Qur'an in chapter 2:37 says Abraham came to God with an undivided or submitted heart i.e. a Muslim heart.

Christians relate to Abraham through faith in Jesus Christ. And this grace/works tension is there in the Scripture for us to see. Galatians 4:21 is an interesting passage where Paul is reacting to this tension. He's come out of the Judaistic line of religious tradition and he says to these Galatians, 'Tell me, you people who want to be under law, don't you understand what the law says? It's written that Abraham had two sons, one from Hagar the slave woman, one from Sarah the freewoman. Ishmael, son of the slave woman, was born according to the flesh' – self effort. 'But Isaac the son of the free woman was born by divine help' – grace. Paul says this is symbolic, for these two are two covenants. The one from Mount Sinai and on Ishmael's side Mount Hirah, where Islam began. Today, we believers in Jesus are children of promise like Isaac. This is the tension, this is the enmity that can be there and we need to address it with our Muslim friends. For we, according to John 3, are 'born from above'. We, like Isaac, are children of promise. Paul continues 'But in the same way as Ishmael, born according to the flesh, persecuted Isaac who was born according to the Spirit . . .' Do you see that tension? Those of the flesh persecuting those of the Spirit. This says something about the reason for the animosity towards Muslims who respond to grace.

Paul says it's just the same now as the Scripture says, 'Cast out the slave woman and her son, for the son of the bondwoman shall not be heir with the son of the free woman.' This grace/works tension has its roots way back in the household of Abraham. 'So then', says Paul, 'we are not children of works, but of grace. Stand firm therefore, in the freedom by which Christ has made us free and don't be entangled again in the yoke of bondage. If you attempt to be acceptable to God through self-effort, you have fallen from grace'. And the grace message is almost totally absent in Islam. To young people, I tell them, your Muslim friends are gagging for grace. Can we be models of grace? Can we have the attraction of grace for inquiring Muslims?

It is more helpful to see a Muslim as an Arabised form of Jew. That's a shock to many Christians. Like Judaism, Islam is rooted in Abraham. It embraces Torah. Are you aware that Shari'a law is a Muslim version of Torah? Islam, as in Judaism, reveres the Old Testament prophets, affirms the Ten commandments; they circumcise their males. They follow a lunar calendar. They have their own kosher food – it's called hallal. They have their own tetrogrammaton, 'There is no God but God and' (I paraphrase) '*our* prophet is his messenger.'

There is almost a Pharisee/Sadducee divide in Sunni/Shi'a Islam. Paul used that very skilfully to get them fighting amongst themselves. You've heard of Muslim brotherhoods. I identify a Jewish brotherhood in Acts 23 where forty Jews covenanted together to kill Paul in the name of God. What about the woman caught in adultery in the Gospels? Jesus walks onto the scene and models a grace response into the very enactment of the law. They were going to stone her to death. Has anyone heard of Amina Lawal in Nigeria? She's under sentence of death by stoning for having a child out of wedlock. Where have they got that from? Straight out of Torah. The challenge if Jesus were here today: what would his response to Amina Lawal be?

In Acts 21, they set upon Paul and beat him for bringing the gospel of grace. Like the Jew, the Muslim is stuck somewhere in the book of Deuteronomy. When you get close enough to a Muslim that they trust you, you'll hear not these words but you'll hear the sentiment coming from their life, 'oh wretched man that I am, who can deliver me from the body of this death?' But they're missing the sentence, 'Thanks be to God through the Prophet 'Isa, I can be set free. I can know Allah.' This exercises my heart tremendously.

If Islam is an Arabised form of Judaism, however pale a reflection, however distorted an image, if it's true, can I suggest to you the approach in witness to Muslims needs to be more of the Old Testament, what we call 'centripetal' witness. To over-simplify, the theme throughout the Old Testament is 'Come, from the nations, to the God of Abraham.' The predominant New Testament theme, 'Go, to the nations, with the God of Abraham.' The one is centripetal – come, *to* the centre. The other is 'centrifugal' which is what your lawn sprinkler does. It goes from the centre to the circumference. That's centrifugal witness. From Jerusalem, Judea, Samaria to the ends of the earth. I've over-simplified because both 'go' and 'come' are in both testaments. But there is a predominance of 'come' in the Old and 'go' in the New. Jesus' references to centripetal witness go like this: 'Come to me, all you who are weary.' That's the Muslim right there.

Jesus said, and this is a motto for witness to Muslims, 'Let your light so shine before men (Muslims), that they may see your good works and glorify your Father in heaven.' Jesus taught centripetal attraction. That's the challenge to our lives. It's not as Os Guinness said 'poor old talkative Christianity.' I've got to win the argument, your doctrine is wrong, mine is superior, I've got to win the argument. We need for Muslims more free samples of the life of Jesus, to be Jesus to them.

Testimony time

I was asked by the secret police in the Middle East to broaden my ministry outside the country and don't come back. A Muslim friend of mine, before I left, said 'Steve, I want to tell you something. You are a better Muslim than I have ever been.' He meant that, like the apostle Paul says, 'You Steve, by nature, are doing the things contained in my book, the law. But what ticks me off is that you're enjoying it.' That because of the indwelling Christ, the grace life.

The Christian attitude to Muslims

Christians and Muslims have an ambivalent attitude to one another. It's based on history, historical kinship and theological kinship links, which many Christians and Muslims wish did not exist. It's rather like the relationship between the Jew and the Samaritan in the Scripture. For the Jew, 'the other lot have an inferior culture to mine. They have a bastardised version of my faith and to top it all, they carry the passport and the legal right of residence in my country.' I see a huge parallel between the Jewish relationship to the Samaritans and the Christian relationship and attitude to Muslims. My colleague, Peter Cotterell, was very honest recently. He served in Africa for many years. He came back to south London. He said he was irritated: 'They've taken over my town!' He came back to Southall, full of Asians – Hindus, Sikhs and Muslims. The next morning he was having a quiet time and the Lord said 'Excuse me, whose town?' The verse in question was 'the earth is the Lord's.' It's no mistake that he's shifting its peoples around. So we have cultural prejudice. There is light and darkness within the Islamic tradition. I actually see a degree of darkness, sadly, within the Christian history as well.

Cultural prejudice – the word of God would have something to say about female circumcision, but God walked with the Jews through the centuries of polygamy and the passing of the death sentence by stoning for sin. These are still practised in some Muslim cultures today. We look down on it.

Political prejudice – Islam can be seen as spiritual communism. Politicised Islam is responsible for many of the armed conflicts going on in the world today. That is irrefutable. Political Islam is less about what's true and more about who's in charge. There are only tenuous links through to the Qur'an for that behaviour. 'Fundamentalist' Islam is, simply put, the use of the ideology of Islam as a tool to achieve a political end.

Theological prejudice – Our attitude is ambivalent or it's confused all the more with the second area: theological compatibility. Muslims are monotheists. They believe in the unity of the one God. They believe in the Torah. They believe in the New Testament as the Injil. They revere Jesus. They believe all the peripherals of Jesus, but seem to deny the two key essentials: his divinity and the cross. There are reasons why they stand where they do. There are also theological contradictions. Genesis 3:8-9 speaks about the voice of the Lord God walking in the garden. I see the whole of Christian and Muslim theology based upon this scene. It is in the bedrock of both. In Christianity and the biblical tradition it shows a God who comes into this world calling for relationship with man. But Islam recoils because it is disrespectful to God. Islam is stuck back there in the Old Testament where you hit the deck for the fear of the Lord. You can't even say his name. There is no personal relationship with God in Islam. A Muslim friend of mine who has come to faith in Christ said it's rather like when I was at school, when you went to see the headmaster, all the house rules were pinned to the headmaster's study door. You didn't go in to interact with him. But now, through the Prophet 'Isa, Jesus, he said the door is flung open and I can go in to the headmaster and know him. For Bilquis Sheikh, the Pakistani lady who wrote *I Dared to Call Him Father*,[1] it was the door being lifted off the hinges. She said, 'I've come

---

[1] Bilquis Sheikh, *I dared to call Him Father* (Eastbourne: Kingsway Communications, 2003)

to know the God I've worshipped from afar all my life. And in Jesus Christ I've come to call him Father.'

Is the God of Islam angry?

We say Islam is angry. It means the God of Islam must be angry. Their God cannot be our God. Allah must be evil. Allah must be behind the anger. Somehow we can't separate out the provocative political issues of an interfering west which make Muslims angry. Perhaps because we're from a colonial society and culture and history, we're less sensitive to how we come over in the two-thirds world. Like we own the place, and rule the place. There's something for us in the west to hear about how we're coming over. The anger is not directly related to the issue of Allah. But I'm going to address it just now as the last cameo.

Is Allah the God of Abraham?

The answer is yes. . . and no. Evidence passed in favour that he is *not* include 'Allah has no son.' He cannot be the God of Abraham. But the God of Abraham in the Old Testament had not yet got a son. Another one is that Allah is violent. Go and read your Old Testament again. Another one is that Allah has ninety-nine names and Father isn't one of them. It proves nothing. Can I just give you some food for thought in what is going to become an increasingly important debate?

Historically, Allah is linked to 'El', the high god of the near east. It was used before Islam, *centuries* before Islam. The name for the high god was Allah amongst Arabic speakers. Linguistically it has a link to the Aramaic 'Elah'. The Hebrew 'alah (God) is the root of El-Elyon, God Most High i.e. the high god. El was used by pagans and refined by the God of the Old Testament through the prophets and through the development of Scripture over centuries. Let's not be afraid of God working with less than satisfactory situations and people. That's where he began with Abraham in an idolatrous, pagan family in Ur of the Chaldeans. Qur'anically, Mohammed referred to God saying 'Our God and your God you Jews our God is one' (Surah 3:84). It is to him that we bow. Mohammed thought that he was referring to the God of the Jews. Pragmatically, where do we go because millions of Christian Arabic speakers have no other name to use. It is the Arabic word for God.

Yes, Allah is the God of Abraham, but the Muslim understanding of him is faulty. Can I quote a very dear man, the Bishop Taqani Tafti of Iran? From a Muslim background, he says, 'Some people tend to think that Muslims have one God and Christians have another. While I agree that the two concepts are very different from each other, I cannot agree that they really worship two utterly different gods. My faith in a Christian God was related to my childhood faith in a Muslim God. When, through the book of Psalms and Job (does that give you any clues in Muslim evangelism?) I learned anew the meaning of trust in God, I came to worship him at the foot of the cross.' Or Phil Parshall, from work in Bangladesh and Asia, says 'Islam presents an inadequate and incomplete but not totally misguided view of God. It seems unfair to say that the God of Islam is absolutely distinct from the God of the Bible.' There are both positives and negatives within Islam. Your attitude to Islam and to Muslims is going to depend on whether, for you, the proverbial glass of Islam is half full or half empty. There's evidence on both sides.

I was speaking at a mission conference recently where a European lady shared a story. She is working in a closed West African country, one of the most closed nations in the world. She met a forty year old woman who had a dream when she was ten years old. In the dream a white woman (something she had never seen), came to the village and gave her a book that would change her life and her religion. Thirty years later, this European lady had the privilege of becoming the woman in the dream. They worked out that the thirty year old European lady was born the same year that the girl had the dream.

Islam and western morality

Don Richardson has said that if a Christian from sixth century Byzantium were to return today they would find more that was familiar to them in the lifestyle and practices of Muslims than in contemporary, western, evangelical Christianity. There's something in that for us in a society where AIDS is romantically ennobled. Mr Blair, the Prime Minister, made the statement, 'Unlike the Taliban and al Qaeda, Britain knows the difference between right and wrong.' Tom Utley, writing for the *Telegraph* said, 'Mr Prime Minister, if Britain knows the difference between right and wrong, why are 3,500 babies aborted every week in this country? Why do footpaths and trees have more rights than the unborn? Why does Britain have the highest teenage pregnancy rate in Europe? Why does Britain have the largest prison population in the western world?'

Khurshid Ahmed, a Muslim commentator, says 'I'd like to invite my western colleagues to understand that Muslim criticism of western civilisation is not primarily an exercise in political confrontation. The real competition is at the level of two cultures and civilisations, one based on Islamic values and the other on the values of materialism and nationalism.' Had western culture been based on Christianity, on morality, on faith, then the language and *modus operandi* would have been very different. But that is not the case. The choice is left between the divine principle which for him is Islam and the secular, materialistic culture.

I have a dream. . .

I have a dream that this country is peopled by Christian men and women and young people who a Muslim can call a *mu'min*, a real believer. That Christians around this country would be to the Muslim neighbours around them like the burning bush. A young lady said to me recently, 'I had a dream of the burning bush and I didn't know the meaning until I listened to your talks. With the burning bush, Moses was attracted by the flames and he came just close enough to hear God call him by name.' Can our lives be like burning bushes to our Muslim neighbours in a very needy western British culture? Can we, with a bit more humility and a Christ-likeness which is attractive, become such a burning bush that draws our Muslim friends into relationship to come just close enough so that through our lives they can hear the divine whisper as God calls them into relationship by name?

Discipleship Isn't For Loners
by Terry Virgo

TERRY VIRGO

Terry is based at the Church of Christ the King, Brighton, and is the leader of Newfrontiers, which is currently serving nearly three hundred churches in twenty-five nations. A well-known Bible teacher, Terry speaks at conferences around the world. He has written several books including *Restoration in the church*, *Enjoying God's grace*, *No well-worn paths* (his autobiography and the story of Newfrontiers) and *Does the future have a church?* He is happily married to Wendy and they have five children and four grandchildren.

Discipleship Isn't For Loners

Introduction

I've been asked to speak on the concept that discipleship is not for loners. And truly that is the case. Discipleship and growing into Christ is a team operation. You and I cannot arrive at maturity alone. I need you, you need me, that we might arrive at the destination. I guess if there is any chapter in the New Testament that describes the summit it is found here in this fourth chapter of Ephesians where Paul is free from problems. He's not trying to address a local problem in a local church. More than in any other epistle, Paul is free in Ephesians to talk about his passion, which I do believe is the church. He speaks of the bride, by implication he speaks of the army, he speaks of the temple. He speaks of the church as the body. He just talks again and again about the church.

Particularly in that thirteenth verse, we read about coming to the unity of the faith, the knowledge of the Son of God, to a mature man, to the measure of the stature which belongs to the fullness of Christ. Imagine coming to the fullness of the stature of Christ, to maturity. That's Paul's goal. He's writing to the people of God together, saying we, together, are to attain to that. That's our goal, that's our objective. God is looking for a mature man, a many-membered man. If you like, Jesus of Nazareth used to be the body of Christ, if I can reverently put it that way. Now we are together the body of Christ; a many-membered body, coming to maturity, together, all around the world, his glorious church. If we're going to arrive there, we need one another. There are over forty 'one another' verses in the New Testament. We have to help one another.

Bearing with one another

I want to pick out three such phrases from the passage that was read for us. The first one is this: bearing with one another. We have to learn to bear with one another. In Ephesians chapter 3, Paul has already spoken about this wonderful, manifold wisdom of God that might now be made known through the church to rulers and authorities in the heavenly places. His concept is that the church is the bright outshining of the glory of God, a prism with his white light shining into it and it becoming multicoloured. So that every tribe and tongue and nation and people, tribes that find it almost impossible to live together, come together in love and harmony; multicoloured, multiracial, multilingual, all coming together only because of one thing: because Jesus has made them one. This is the way God will be greatly glorified, not only in the world in terms of missionary application but somehow as a demonstration to the rulers and the authorities. Like God saying, 'Look what I can do in this broken, fractious society where men hate one another. Look what I can do. Look what my Son has accomplished.'

It's the church that's going to show off the greatness and the grace of God. It's a multicoloured show. God has that objective in view. He is accomplishing that. Through history, through our generation he is doing that more and more as the gospel goes out. He will have a glorious mature church. And in Ephesians 3, the first three chapters, he's setting out the doctrine, the ideals. He's told us what his goal is. But in Ephesians 4:1 he begins to say, 'Therefore, brothers' and as is the case in many of the epistles, there is a kind of turning point. Having said that's the objective, now he says, 'You start living this out. It's for you to accomplish these things.' And the way into this wonderful picture that he's painting is for you and I, first of all, to bear with one another.

God is going to do this great thing, but he's going to use very diverse people, people who wouldn't normally be able to cope with one another. The early church started like that, with Jews and Greeks; Jews with their very religious background; a very locked up lifestyle. Now they've found Christ. They can hardly imagine the liberty. Then the gospel goes out to pagan nations where they know nothing of that lifestyle and they've found Christ. Somehow these people, so vastly different, have to come together and be one people. The Greeks with their gods and their strange ways, the Jews with their rigid religion, coming together and forming one new man. It's an extraordinary thing!

Then there were slaves and free men. Slaves were objects that other people possessed. They had no identity, personality, privileges. They were just things. Now they were sons of God. And they're in the same house church with wealthy people, who owned them. Now you're brothers, now you're together. Imagine coming together across that great social divide. Male and female; the gospel gave new freedom, honour, dignity to women. They were all gathered in. It wasn't as though they all came from the same background. Their traditions, expectations, lifestyles were hugely different. They were to come together and display the wonder of Christ. How can you do that? You start by bearing with one another.

We have to be good at putting up with one another. It's the way in. It's the stepping stone into the great vision. We're going to arrive at the fullness of the stature of Christ. Putting up with one another is how we start. How do I learn to put up with you? How do you learn to put up with me? Because we have got all these divisions; class divisions; age divisions; increasingly a division between the old and the young; race divisions, still the male/female challenges. We have huge challenges to be won, to be a people that dwell in love.

. . .with humility

How do we bear with one another? The key is to have a right attitude to ourselves. It's in the text. It says, '. . . with humility, with gentleness and with patience.' Don't put requirements on one another. We start with a humble attitude to ourselves. If you are full of pride, you will have difficulty relating to others. If you have certain requirements of other people before you accept them, that's the end. We have to start with that humble attitude. Apparently Winston Churchill said of Attlee, 'He's a very humble man, but he has much to be humble about.' The reality is that we also have much to be humble about. As we come to God and often as we pray our prayers and ask God for mercy and forgiveness, we need to carry the attitude we often have before God on our knees into our relationships with one another. We're looking for a humility, a lowliness of mind.

It's something very foreign to the culture into which Paul wrote. Armitage Robinson says in his commentary, 'To the Greek mind, humility was little else than a vice of nature.' It was weak and mean-spirited. Their attitude to life was that a man owed to himself self-respect. That creeps into our age with its road rage and its anger and its willingness to assert. God says, if you're going to come into the church, you leave that self assertion outside and you come in with lowliness, realizing you only get in by his immense mercy and kindness. We've nothing to be proud of and as we take that lowly stance, we'll learn how to bear with one another. We'll live on that level ground with lowliness. Romans 12 says '. . . don't be high-minded . . .' Some people say 'I don't suffer fools gladly'. That really just means 'I'm easily irritated.' We've to learn to bear with one another by having a lowly view of ourselves.

. . .with gentleness

Do you make it easy for people to draw near? Jesus said 'I am meek and lowly of heart. Come to me and you'll find rest.' Do people find rest when they come to you? Do they meet a lowly heart? The Greek is the word *prous*. It's the word that's being used when a horse is being broken in. Sometimes in Western movies there's a horse that can't be broken in. No one can ride it until John Wayne comes along. He gets on and the horse is gradually *prous*. It's gentle. What does that mean? That it can't run fast any more? It's got no more strength? It means it doesn't kick back any more. It's gentle, it's broken in. Some people say brokenness is the whole Christian message and the most godly Christians are totally destroyed people. I don't believe that's what it's about. But, a broken and a contrite heart God won't despise. He wants us to have a heart that's broken in, a non-retaliatory heart. When reviled, they don't revile again. Spoken against, written against, criticized, harshly referred to, you don't find a 'fight back' in them. Somehow they've got through that. That's in history. They've had dealings with God. They walk in the fear of the Lord.

When we've got through that, we find it easier to bear with one another. Bearing with other people has a lot to do with things already having happened in you because of your relationship with Jesus. It makes you a better team member. Because we're together, there is a brokenness about us. Moses was the meekest man in all the earth. Now does that mean he was weak? I've just been reading how Moses came down that mountain and found they'd made the golden calf. He was furious with them, he broke the tablets. It says he took the golden calf, made them grind it to dust, put it in water and made them drink it. You think, this is the meekest man in all the earth?! But this time God's glory is at stake. On another occasion, when Aaron and Miriam come up to him and say, 'Who do you think you are, Moses?' there is no defence. When the sons of Korah come to him and say 'Moses, we're all holy', Moses doesn't defend himself. He says, 'Be careful.' He's concerned for them. But he doesn't defend himself. There's a meekness. He's the meekest man in all the earth. Do you have a meekness in your heart because you've met the meek and lowly Jesus? Has something happened to you? You say 'I speak straight. I'm Joe Blunt. Take me as you find me. I'm honest.' Hey brother, that won't do. You may feel it's honest, but it's not like Jesus. We've got to move on from that, to a place where God deals with us and there's a meekness in us.

. . .with patience

Paul is giving us the clues how to do it. Love is patient. It's lovely having grandchildren. It's a new experience for us in the last couple of years. When you've had enough, you say to your child, 'Here's your child. Smells a bit. Over to you.' It's such fun. We're going through that stage where they're beginning to walk. The Bible says so plainly in 1 Corinthians 13, 'Love is patient.' It just is. That's just the characteristic of love. So you see a little child, it tries to walk, takes a step and down it goes. It takes another step and down it falls and you don't say, as a parent, 'Listen, if you can't walk, walk in two years' time and do it then.' You don't say that as a parent. You say, 'Come on, get up, have another go.' I remember teaching my children to walk. Love is patient. It just is.

We've to learn to be patient. 'Oh but he messed me up.' Yeah. 'She spoke something...' Yeah. Are you communicating patience? Love is patient. Love doesn't retaliate quickly. We bear with one another with patience. The word means long-tempered, not short-tempered. Christians should be excellent at one thing. You may be bad at witnessing, you may find prayer difficult, understanding the Bible... All kinds of things can be difficult, but one thing we should all excel at is forgiving one another. We should be brilliant at it.

Take mercy. I give away mercy all the time. Pray the prayer regularly. Father forgive me as I forgive. Live with the easy giving away of forgiveness. Why? Look at the context. Paul says it's because we're to be diligent to preserve the unity of the Spirit. There's something amazingly precious that's been deposited with us. We have a unity, it's not one we've arrived at in terms of theological agreement. We'll arrive at that later. It talks about attaining 'to' the unity of the faith. That's something we strive towards as we speak the truth. We start with a unity which has come down out of heaven. It's the Spirit's unity.

When Peter went to Cornelius' household, he was very scared. He was going into the home of a Gentile dog, beyond his normal sphere of feeling safe. He wondered what the other apostles would think. And he shares the gospel, and while he's sharing the gospel the Spirit fell upon Cornelius and his household. Peter said, 'God gave them the Spirit like he did to us!' And when he got back with the other apostles, Peter's on the carpet. They're saying to him 'What are you doing eating with Gentiles?' Peter says, 'While I spoke to them, the Spirit came on them, like he did on us.' 'Oh! It's God then? Who are we to withstand God?' They had a unity which didn't come through negotiation, through swapping papers with one another, it came through God. And they said, 'who are we to withstand God?' They had a unity because of the Holy Spirit.

Sometimes we use that word 'spirit' rather carelessly: 'There was a nice spirit in that meeting.' 'That guy has such a nice spirit.' Here it means the unity which the Holy Spirit gives. It's a unity that is God-given and churches – local churches and then groups of churches – should put a high price on maintaining that unity because the Bible seems to suggest the Spirit can be grieved. He's a personality, he has a gentleness about him. There's something about the Spirit, he's looking for respect. He's looking for peace, where he can dwell. He's looking for unity and he will withdraw where he sees disunity, hatred and backbiting. You can go into churches and you can think 'Boy, it's cold here.' And you can go to churches and you can think, 'Wow, heaven is here.' The presence of God…You and I have a huge responsibility because this unity is a God-given thing. It's sovereign. It's the Spirit that gives us unity. We have to work hard to maintain that unity.

. . . make every effort

Marcus Sparks says, in his commentary on Ephesians, 'It's hardly possible to render exactly the urgency contained in the Greek verb.' Not 'She knows my phone number if she wants to get it right.' 'He knows where I live. He started it, he can get it right.' No. Make every effort. Be diligent. John Stott says in his commentary, 'It's a call to continuous, diligent activity.'[1] Have you overstepped with anybody? You say, 'We've not fellowshipped for a long time.' You can even go to churches where people haven't spoken for a long time, where people have resentful attitudes. As though that will do in the house of God! As though that's acceptable. It says 'make every effort.' How are you going to answer to Jesus when the Bible is saying, 'Be diligent'? You have to be urgent. We need to be diligent to bear with one another; with lowliness, humility, patience, jealously guarding a context where the Spirit can be present, and at home with us. I long for my generation to see God's church in all her beauty. While we're content to be out of step with our brother, our sister, not making every effort to put it right, we're not jealously looking for the presence of the Spirit. We need to be very diligent,

---

[1] J.W.R. Stott, *The Message of Ephesians* (Leicester: IVP)

bearing with one another. Have a lowly attitude to yourself. That's the
starting place.

Speak the truth in love

Doctrine

I believe there are two possible ways of reading this. It could be, speaking the doctrine, which is probably the more likely one given the
context, because it says 'don't be tossed about like children, by every
wind of doctrine. But speak the truth in love . . .' 'Beware the danger
of doctrinal error' seems to be the context. We do need to speak the
truth. Some people say, 'Doctrine is the greatest enemy of the church,
it just divides.' That is a silly mistake. We have to have truth. It's the
truth that makes you free. We've got to keep speaking the truth, but
we do it in love. We speak the doctrine to one another in love. The
way we're going to attain to unity is to keep speaking the doctrine to
one another. We mustn't back off doctrine as though doctrine was an
enemy. We have to attain to unity by speaking the truth to one
another. We have to share the truth.

There are different ways of sharing truth. When I was at
London Bible College, I was quite a young Christian. I was
exposed to the Calvinistic wing and the Arminian wing at London
Bible College. They used to 'share the doctrine' with one another.
It was a bit like McEnroe and Connors sharing a tennis ball. 'What
about this verse and what about this verse? You must be joking!'
Horrific sharing of truth with one another; aggressive use of the
Bible which never brings unity. We can share the truth honestly.
We can share when people are thirsty, hungry, willing, open to
learn. We've to share the truth. In James 3:17 it says, 'The wisdom
from above is gentle, reasonable, peaceable, willing to yield' it says
in the margin in this translation. Yet it goes on to say, 'unwavering'. How can you be unwavering and willing to yield at the same
time? It calls for maturity. We should, as believers, tend to be rock-
like. You say, 'these are things I believe. I'm unwavering, but if you
can show me . . .'

I mentioned earlier that when I'd been a Christian for years, suddenly, in a new way, I saw the grace of God, the acceptance of God, the thrill of knowing Jesus is my righteousness. He's the same yesterday, today and for ever. I don't have to produce a righteousness of my own to be acceptable. When I wake up in the morning Jesus is my righteousness before I've tried to pray for ages or read my Bible for hours. Jesus is going to be my righteousness tomorrow morning when I wake up, and every morning when I wake up for ever. Hallelujah!

He's my righteousness. That set me free. I don't have to earn points. Jesus has done it for me. Now that was a breakthrough in my thinking. Other things, like eschatology, change your thinking. About church, you change your thinking. The working of the Spirit, you change your thinking. If people can share truth with love, you can say 'that's something I've not seen before.' We don't have to see it as threatening. We can see that's helping us up the path. We must do it, but we must do it with love. John Stott says, 'Truth becomes hard if it's not softened by love. And love becomes soft if it's not strengthened by truth.'

Or it could be that Paul is speaking about simply being truthful. Again in the same chapter, verse 25, it says, 'lay aside falsehood.' Speak truthfully; seeing, he says, 'you are members of one another.' What he's saying is this, if you lie to a member of the same body, it's foolishness. If eye lies to foot and doesn't say there's something down there and just tells you 'it's plain sailing', then you trip and fall. The problem is we're all the same body. Don't lie to one another. You are members of one another. It's going to bounce back on you. You are integrally joined together. It's stupid to lie to one another.

Christians rarely invent lies. Very rarely will a Christian think, 'What lie shall I think up today?' But we are vulnerable to exaggeration, generalization, just expanding things. 'She's always doing it', means she did it once before. 'Everybody's talking about it' means you heard someone mention it. If you've been a pastor for any length of time you will know about having to unravel situations. You take it back and back, and you'll find a point where someone exaggerated. We've got to stop being careless with words. We must speak the truth, jealously guarding the truth. Sometimes we have to say hard things to one another, but in love. It's God's goal for us. It's how we're going to arrive. Discipleship is not for loners. You will never grow to maturity alone. He's looking for a holy community. And we need one another. We need people to say to us, 'I need to say to you, when you are with your wife, you don't honour her. Sometimes when you're in company, you cut her off in conversation.' Do you have anyone close enough to you to say that to you? 'I don't expect anyone to say anything like that to me!' How are we going to arrive at maturity together unless you've got a friend close enough to help you through? We need one another, we'll never arrive without one another.

Building up the body

Verse 16, it says, 'the whole body being fitted and held together by what every joint supplies according to the proper working of each individual part causes the growth of the body for the building up of itself.' Paul doesn't even say 'building up one another' there. His concept of the body of Christ is so developed that he talks about building up itself. He means really building up one another. It's quite plain that's what he means. But he sees us corporately so much. We have this excessive individualism about our Christianity. We interpret every New Testament command as though it was just to me.

In English there is no distinction between you in singular and you in plural. And we tend to read all the 'yous' as singular when most of them are plural. There's something we must do together. It's together we arrive, it's together that we develop. We need to be together. It says of the early church they were together. Do you notice that in Acts chapter 2, 3, 4, they were together. Someone said the early church lived together and then daily went out into the world, and occasionally went to church. The context of our lives tends to be secular. Secular values, secular context, individually trying to walk with God.

For me one of the biggest shocks of my life was when I got saved out of a very ungodly background. My parents were not Christian and I had no godly upbringing and I grew up with a group of fellows. We often got drunk together, we went partying a lot together. We were very close friends. There wasn't anything we wouldn't talk about to one another. We shared secrets with one another. Then I got saved and got into the church and lost all my friends. I couldn't find much friendship in church. I would say the sense of community I enjoyed with the group of young men I grew up with was far superior to the level of community that I found at church. I went to what would have been regarded as a good, big church, Baptist church, six hundred members, wonderful preacher. Always blessed me. Godly, lovely man. But it was very hard to feel integrated. You met the dear pastor at the door, shook his hand, said 'Goodbye. See you next Sunday'. But I had Monday, Tuesday, Wednesday, Thursday, Friday and Saturday to live through without sinning, which was tough. I needed some friends, someone I could get close to, I needed to be together with others or the pull of the world was far too great. If I went with my old friends, that meant sinning. I had to get into the church. We're going to find that more and more as we reach out. As you use *Alpha*, or whatever it is you're using, you'll get someone who sees the gospel, but it's not just knowing Jesus, it's a lifestyle they need to be taken out of. It's not enough to say we'll be there next Sunday. They've got to have someone they can cling to. We will build one another when we are together. We have to be together in one another's homes, not just at the church building. That's what God wants. We've got to get beyond normal, historic expectations of simply being 'a twice on Sunday man.' We've got to be into one another's homes, into one another's lives, sharing, loving.

Every part working properly

Again to quote John Stott, 'The New Testament envisages not a single pastor with a docile flock, but both a plural oversight and an every member ministry.' I used to visit a lady in the first pastorate I was involved in as a young man out of college. She had a stroke and was in a wheelchair. One side of her body was useless. She was bright, but she was limited because she had some useless members. Paul is saying, 'I want every part working properly, equipping the saints for the work

of their ministry.' We're not to be passive. We're not just to be enter-
tained. 'What's your ministry?' 'My ministry? I go along.' It's to be
every part working properly. We need to be being discipled. We need
churches full of training in all kinds of things. Not just training for
how to take up the communion or the offering. There are other things
to be trained in: working with the poor, working in kids' clubs, invad-
ing whole housing estates, serving people whose lives are destroyed,
getting them off drugs. There are all kinds of ministries. What's your
part?

In the body you know what the parts are for. It's one of the ways
you grow up. A baby doesn't know what the parts are for. A baby just
lies there in the cot. Sometimes they see their hand. 'I wonder what's
that for?' They don't realize it's joined on. They think toes are for
sucking and knees are for walking on. But that's an immature baby.
They don't know what the bits are for. But when a child grows up it
begins to learn, 'Feet are for walking!' How do I find what the ministry of this hand is? The hand finds it's good at doing up buttons,
combing hair and blowing noses. You serve the body and you find
what you're there for. You find your gift. Find how you serve the body.
You'll gradually find out what you're good at because the appreciation of the body grows. The body grows into maturity, every part
working properly. Are you bearing with one another? Even in your
marriage, are you bearing with one another? Parents and children,
those kids in the church, are you bearing with them? Have a lowly
heart; gentle; patient. Are you speaking the truth? Are you diligent to
speak it with love? Are you diligent to make sure you don't pass on
anything? We can damage people so much, jump to conclusions, not
caring. The Spirit of God is withdrawing. Another dead church,
another building closes; our nation looks and says 'Our historic religion is fading away.' Does the future have a church? People are asking.
I read in *The Times* our national religion is fading fast. One thousand
church buildings are expected to close in the next fifteen years. Are
we caring? Holy Spirit, help us to walk with you.

The Holy Spirit in Discipleship

by Steve Brady

STEVE BRADY

Steve was converted in his teens in Liverpool and trained at London Bible College, during which time he met and married Brenda. They have two children, Paul and Ruth, and a grandson, Daniel. Steve held pastorates in Leicester, London and Bournemouth before becoming Principal of Moorlands Bible College, which trains men and women for Christian service at home and overseas. His preaching has taken him to conferences and conventions throughout the UK and abroad. Steve serves on the councils of the Evangelical Alliance and the Keswick Convention, and is a member of the Tyndale Fellowship. He is a keen sportsman and hates gardening!

SUMMARY

The Holy Spirit in Discipleship

Introduction

I'd like you to turn with me to 1 Thessalonians. Paul is writing to this comparatively young church. They're trying to work out what it means to be a Christian. They haven't had much input directly from the apostle. Now he's writing to them to try and build them up. Turn to 1 Thessalonians 4. This is an encouragement to every preacher; 'Finally, brother . . .', then he goes on for another two chapters.

> Finally brothers (and sisters), we instructed you how to live in order to please God, as in fact you are living. Now we ask you and urge you in the Lord Jesus to do this more and more. For you know what instructions we gave you by the authority of the Lord Jesus. It is God's will that you should be sanctified: that you should avoid sexual immorality; that each of you should learn to control his own body in a way that is holy and honourable, not in passionate lust like the heathen, who do not know God; and that in this matter no-one should wrong his brother or take advantage of him. The Lord will punish men for all such sins, as we have already told you and warned you. For God did not call us to be impure, but to live a holy life. Therefore, he who rejects this instruction does not reject man but God, who gives you his Holy Spirit. Brothers,

we do not want you to be ignorant... (the word there is where we get the English word agnostic – Brothers, I do not want you to be agnostic...) ...about those who fall asleep, or to grieve like the rest of men, who have no hope. We believe that Jesus died and rose again and so we believe that God will bring with Jesus those who have fallen asleep in him. According to the Lord's own word, we tell you that we who are still alive, who are left till the coming of the Lord, will certainly not precede those who have fallen asleep. For the Lord himself will come down from heaven, with a loud command, with the voice of the archangel and with the trumpet call of God, and the dead in Christ will rise first. After that, we who are still alive and are left will be caught up together with them in the clouds to meet the Lord in the air. And so we will be with the Lord for ever. Therefore, encourage each other with these words.

Then from verse 12 of chapter 5:

Now we ask you brothers, to respect those who work hard among you, who are over you in the Lord and who admonish you. Hold them in the highest regard in love because of their work. Live in peace with each other. And we urge you brothers, warn those who are idle, encourage the timid, help the weak, be patient with everyone. Make sure that nobody pays back wrong for wrong, but always try to be kind to each other and to everyone else. Be joyful always; pray continually; give thanks in all circumstances, for this is God's will for you in Christ Jesus. Do not put out the Spirit's fire; do not treat prophecies with contempt. Test everything. Hold on to the good. Avoid every kind of evil.

Last August, my wife and I were celebrating our twenty-seventh wedding anniversary. We went down to see a live version of *Singing in the Rain*. They actually warn you, when you come along make sure you bring plastic macs, and they provide them for those who are in the front row. There's a big water trough there, and halfway through, down comes all this water and the folk in the front row get wet. All the folk at the front are getting wet, and singing in the rain, having a great time, lots of applause. Then we came out about 10 o'clock and the heavens had opened. As I looked around at all these people, they didn't look like they were singing anymore. As soon as they hit the real rain, they stopped singing. And I thought there might be a sermon illustration in this. I've been to lots of services where we've sung some incredible things: 'We've got a mighty God', and 'God's at work in us, his purpose to perform', and then we get outside, the kids are playing up, the wife's playing up, and we're playing up, and we're not singing any more.

The Spirit of God is, among all the other things, the Spirit of song. He is the Spirit of joy, and of grace to help us in our time of need. We must never forget when we are talking about the Spirit of God, we are talking about a person. He is a person who feels, who thinks. The Bible talks about the mind of the Spirit. He testifies, he guides, he loves, he's a person. In fact he is God the Holy Spirit. And because he's the most mysterious member of the triune God, he's sometimes described like a wind. Other times he's described like a dove — gentle. So we're told not to grieve the Spirit. You can damage this pulpit, but you can't grieve it; it's an inanimate object. You can grieve a person and he can be grieved, according to Ephesians 4:30.

Here in this passage, we're told, verse 19, 'Do not put out the Spirit's fire'. Do not, literally, quench the Spirit. Do not hinder him, do not restrain him, do not suppress him. Do not stifle him. Never dampen, says one translation, the fire of the Spirit. The Spirit of God is given so that you may sing in the rain no matter what the circumstances. The Spirit of God is given so that Christ may be formed in you. The Spirit of God is given not just so that you are informed better, but that you are transformed, that you become a person who is being changed into the image of Christ. One of the great problems for many of us is that we proclaim change loudly, don't we? And then we see so little of it. How many Californians does it take to change a light bulb? Fifteen, one to change it and fourteen to enjoy the experience. How many Liverpudlians does it take to change a light bulb? Twenty; one to hold the light bulb, the other nineteen to turn the ceiling. And of all people on planet earth we believe in the greatest change of all, so we don't want to be in a rut. The wonderful thing about the Spirit is that he comes, and he is the change agent. He is Christ by the Spirit at work in us, to change us, to form us, to transform us, to make us different, to make us new, to make us all that we are positionally in Christ, in reality. So that one day when we stand before him we shall be like Jesus. That's why Paul says in this passage, do not dampen the Spirit's fire.

I want to tell you how to quench the Spirit of God, in the context of these verses here in 1 Thessalonians.

Develop spiritual naiveté

Notice how Paul balances it, 'Do not put out the Spirit's fire; do not treat prophecies with contempt. Test everything. Hold on to the good. Avoid every kind of evil.' When we come to these verses, it all depends where you're coming from. None of us comes to Scripture, if we've been reading it for a while, without bringing some of our own lenses and frameworks, and the like. It's our baggage. In other words, it's how you interpret Scripture and the truth is we all have our filters on. When it talks here about prophecy, some of us immediately, depending where we're coming from, say 'we know what that means, some of those wide-eyed characters saying "thus saith the Lord" and all that nonsense stuff. Don't they know the canon of Scripture is closed?' All of us have heard some absolutely lunatic prophecies, haven't we? Remember in 1976, the year of the great drought? One of my friends told me that he'd heard a prophecy to the effect that there was never going to be any more rain. So there are some of us who despise anything that has a sense of immediacy. There are others of us who want an immediate word from God. The Bible's OK, but, you know, if somebody stands up in a meeting and says, 'thus saith the Lord, I want you to love each other' they think 'God's told us to love each other. That's really direct isn't it?' Well, yes it is, but he did say it in the Bible too, didn't he?

I think what we've got to understand is this: that we've got the word of God. We've got a closed canon of Scripture. Does that mean that God's all closed up and can't say anything immediate to us in terms of immediate application? I don't think it means that at all. We're told here not to despise prophesying. Let me give you some quotes from one or two well-known names, if I can. This is what

Professor Don Carson says, 'The prophecy Paul has in mind is revelatory, and Spirit-prompted . . . and it may . . . deal largely with questions of application of gospel truth . . . None of this means it is necessarily authoritative, infallible or canon-threatening.'[1]

This is what John Stott says, 'There are today secondary and subsidiary kinds of prophetic gifts and end-time ministries. For God undoubtedly gives to some a remarkable degree of insight either into Scripture itself and its meaning, or into its application to the contemporary world, or into his particular will for particular people in particular situations.'[2] That's interesting for some of us who so jealously want to guard the finality and canonicity of Scripture that God has spoken. We are not threatening the canon of Scripture. But God can, in his mercy, turn up... We heard from Charles this morning, about a person who is not a Christian, who hears a voice from nowhere saying, 'go to church.' That person comes along to church and begins to hear the gospel. Do you seriously believe that God can say that to a non-Christian but he couldn't possibly say to one of his people, 'I want you to do that'?

I'm trying to be as objective as I can. Perhaps the best illustration is like this. If we are wise Christians we do not despise prophesying but we test, it says, everything. We test it by what God said. Will you check it out with other believers? Will you say, 'What do you think of that?' You weigh it and you sift it. And there isn't a Christian, whatever our title, whether we're cessationist, charismatic, reformed, non-charismatic, it doesn't matter what our label is, there's not a Christian who does not have God, in some remarkable ways by his Spirit because he's the sovereign Spirit, breaking into their lives. Probably the most non-charismatic Christian I know. . . I was in a real dilemma about something. I bumped into him at a minister's meeting and he knew nothing about what was on my heart and he said, 'I can't stop. I've got to catch a train, but I'm telling you from the Lord, don't

---

[1] D.A. Carson, *Showing the Spirit* (Grand Rapids: Baker Book House, 1987), p163

[2] J.R.W. Stott, *The Message of Thessalonians* (Leicester: Inter-Varsity Press, 1991), p128

do it!' I thought, 'God, if you got it through him this really must be serious. I'm listening!'

Have you ever seen those guys in London, who drive around with those flip boards on scooters? They're would-be taxi drivers, wandering all around London, 'doing the knowledge' so that they have this mind map in their heads and then eventually they become taxi drivers. And if they're wise taxi drivers, because London is always changing, one-way streets appear and new housing estates come, then you continue to do the knowledge. God has given us his word. If we're sound and wise Christians, we get into this book. Doesn't God break in as we walk with him? There are times when he breaks in and says, 'I want you to do that'. Here we're being encouraged not to be spiritually naïve. So we're not going to be suckered by every wild-eyed prophecy on the one side, nor are we going to be so closed up so that God himself cannot get through and speak to us. Professor Neil Hood was signing some books yesterday and he was explaining how at 3 o'clock in the morning, God had woken him up and just laid on his heart that, although he's a leading academic in his business field, he was to give his time to writing Christian books to help the church. If you want to quench the Spirit just develop spiritual naïveté. Either believe nothing or believe everything.

Settle for church mediocrity

Now these are verses 12 to18 and this would take a whole pile of time to do any justice to them. Verses 16–18 gives us just these short things: 'Be joyful always.' This is a command. It's not just when you feel like it. There are times when we've got to be joyful. But it's not just on your face, it's something in your heart. It's the joy of the Spirit coming. It says don't stifle him. Be joyful always.

One day I bumped into this guy and he was having a bad day. I mean, everything was wrong with the church and every other version of the Bible but the one he used. He said 'just around the corner from where I go to church there is a big Baptist church. About a thousand people come out on a Sunday looking happy. Smiling.' I asked him,

'How do you come out of your church then?' He said, 'We come out of our church beating our chests, mourning our sins, bemoaning our total depravity.' I had no doubts that he was right. So I thought I ought to give him a divine version. 'Didn't the apostle Peter speak about joy unspeakable and full of glory being a mark of a Christian?' And this miserable face looked at me and said, 'But it's *unspeakable* joy.'

Here Paul says be joyful, be prayerful. These are plurals again. Churches that are in touch with the Spirit. Somebody said that if you want to know how popular a preacher is, go on a Sunday morning. If you want to know how popular a church is, go on Sunday night and if you want to know how popular Jesus is, go to the mid-week prayer meeting. We need to learn to pray more. There's a whole world of need out there. That's the one thing that slips off the agenda. We have to be creative, because folk are under pressure.

He talks also about being thankful. There are a lot of bitter people around. They don't have an attitude of gratitude. Now we live in a tough world, I know that. He says, giving thanks not *for* or *under* all circumstances, giving thanks *in* all circumstances. Why? '*Because through all the changing scenes in life, in trouble and the joy; the praises of my God may still my heart and tongue employ.*' God doesn't change, so when I'm having a bad day, God has not vacated his throne, God's plans and purposes for his church and me are still on track. Hallelujah! So I can be grateful to God that he is still working out his purposes in me and through me. The Spirit of God is a positive Spirit.

In the most absurd circumstances I face, if I'm in touch with the Spirit of grace, I know this: 'God moves in a mysterious way.' You don't have to be under the circumstances, you are *in* the circumstances by the grace and permission of a sovereign God. That's why Paul says you can be thankful, you can be joyful, you can be prayerful, no matter what. Off the back of that, the verses before talk about the people of God. Don't settle for church mediocrity when it's doom and gloom time. Every time we get together we're the tough brigade. 'Do you know what they're going to do to us from Europe?' The Lord God almighty is still reigning. Maybe we do need a shake-up from Europe, to wake us out of this sloth of death. God may come and revive his work, and he often does that by pain, suffering, setback and sometimes persecution. Let's not settle for church mediocrity. Verses 12 through 15 give us a lovely picture of being part of God's new society. We're a colony of the kingdom in space, time, history. So if you're going to do church, honour your leaders. Go back and encourage your spiritual leaders. They're among you, because they're brothers and sisters, whatever your leadership functions and ways of doing things are. Also they watch for your souls, as Hebrews 13 puts it. And then he says, you've got to help each other in the people of God. It's not just holding them in the highest regard because of their work.

And we urge you, brothers, warn those who are idle. Do you know any idle people in your church? It's the tercentenary of the birth of John Wesley, born in 1703. This is what he wrote at eighty-six. 'Laziness is slowly creeping in. There's a tendency to stay in bed after 5.30 in the morning.' Encourage those who are idle. Just say, 'You know, brother, I think you could be doing more.' You don't have to say 'in love', they'll know if it's in love or not. At least I always do.

'. . . encourage the timid'. Do you know what timid means? It means, literally, 'the little soul' who are seeing problems everywhere. Have you folk like that in your church? Grace wants to turn little souls into brave hearts. That's what the Spirit does. He's a great transformer. And what about the weak? This is a word that has a wide range of meaning; the physically weak, the spiritually weak, it's a catch-all. Those who are weak in the church. Not everybody's got it together. Some folk see giants everywhere. I remember there was a man who used to come every week when I was a pastor in east London. He always had problems. Every week he'd be along. 'How've you been this week, Jimmy?' I'd ask. He'd say, 'I've been down in the dumps.' Jimmy did more for my counselling ability and skills than anybody I've known. One week he came to me and I asked him, 'How are you doing, Jimmy?' He said, 'I'm feeling better now, Pastor.' I said, 'I'm so glad to hear that Jimmy', thinking my counselling is working. 'Why is that?' 'I've been going to see this other pastor, every week for the last eight years. I've just heard he's moving.' 'Aren't you sad about that?' 'Oh no, all that counselling has been wearing me out.' And I love this phrase: 'Be patient with everyone.' It's loving your neighbour.

Forget your destiny

Chapter 4:13 to 5:11, I'm just giving you the headlines here. We used to sing in the old days, didn't we, 'This world is not my home, I'm just a-passing through . . .' We don't sing that a lot now, do we? Somewhere over the last twenty-five, thirty years or more, the church has lost her eschatology. We've forgotten we're a pilgrim people, a people of destiny. That this world is something we use just for a while and in Jesus Christ, the best of all, is yet to come. We have to be very careful how we handle prophecy. If we forget prophecy we lose perspective, we forget our destiny. Now I haven't time to expand these verses in any way at all, except to say that the big picture that emerges here, especially in chapter 4, reminds us that the Lord is coming back. The return of the Lord himself, verse 16, do you see that? He's not sending a committee, this is the second coming. The Lord himself will come down from heaven. It will be the resurrection of the dead, the rapture of the saints, the reunion of the church. So we will be for ever with the Lord. Your future is bright because your future is the Lord Jesus himself.

I shall see him face to face. Have you ever thought of that? The whole purpose for your redemption, the whole story line of Scripture from Genesis to Revelation is how the sons of ignorance and night may dwell in eternity and light. And his servant, the book of Revelation says, shall see his face. Some of you are getting on in years. Your best is yet to come. My best years are still in the future because they are sealed with the blood of Christ for ever. Then we'll run and not be weary, walk and not faint. There is coming a day when God will wipe away every tear from our eyes

This is birthed in us by the Spirit. You're caught between two ages when you become a Christian. The Spirit of God comes into your life. He's the foretaste, says Scripture, of what's to be. He puts a little bit of heaven in our hearts by his Spirit to take us home to heaven on. But we're not there yet. We're trapped between the ages. We've got the now. We're in Christ, we're redeemed, we're being saved, being changed. But one day in all its fullness we will be saved. 'Now we will be beginning', says the last chapter of *The Last Battle* of C.S. Lewis' Narnia, 'the Chapter One of the Great story, which no one on earth

has read . . . in which every chapter is better than the one before.'
That's heaven, that's the eternal state, the new heaven and earth
wherein righteousness dwells.

Abandon Christian charity

If you want to grieve the Spirit of God, abandon Christian charity, that's
verses 9-12. And this is what Paul says, 'Now about brotherly love,' verse
9 'we do not need to write to you, for you yourselves have been taught
by God to love each other.' Could that be said of your church? Is love
a kind of optional extra? We're to speak the truth in love. Jesus was full
of grace and truth. He was full of both. It's a terrible thing to go to
churches where love is an add-on extra. They're sound, but soundly
asleep. They're orthodox but ossified. Some Christians seem to have had
a personality bypass when it comes to love. They're faultily faultless, icily
correct. No burning heart for Jesus and they would never lift a finger
to help their church members or their neighbours.

He says you're the community where love is manifest, in manifold
supply. It's part of letting your light so shine before men. And that's what
he talks about in the marketplace in verse 12. He says, 'so that your daily
life may win the respect of outsiders and so that you'll not be depend-
ent on anybody.' This is people living out their lives before the gaze of
a cynical, harsh world and the world saying 'There's something different about you.' They see your good works and glorify your Father in
heaven. The good works are also matched with good words. You live the
life but you also speak the truth, you share the gospel. And then they
put two and two together. They're not just hearing the radio programme or just seeing a TV programme without any sound. They're
seeing sound and pictures; that'll grip. And he says, if you want to grieve
and quench the Spirit, why not abandon Christian charity.

Compromise personal purity

Finally, chapter 4:1-8, specifically here he's talking about sexual
purity. And which one of us hasn't had problems in that area? God's

created this wonderful gift, which is everywhere trammelled in the mud. I've got to tell you nothing binds and blinds us more, though it's not the worst of sins, than blowing it in this area. Some of us always are trying to see how far we can go without getting our fingers burned. We don't set right boundaries.

We're in a sex mad world. There's an incredibly close relationship between spirituality and sexuality. The very part of our brain that seems to be the area where our spirituality is expressed, is the very same part of our brain where our sexuality seems to be expressed. That's why in the Song of Solomon it's hard to know whether it's sexual or spiritual. And sometimes people think the more spiritual I am the less sexual I'm going to be. That actually isn't so. But if you want to quench the Spirit of God's work in your life, compromise personal purity. Some of us blokes, we really struggle. Every day we get offers. They come to us over the web, down our e-mails or whatever. The porn industry has a bigger turnover than tobacco, alcohol and drugs combined. Women are exploited and children are exploited. And Christians by the thousands are bombed out in this area. Notice what Paul says, 'It is God who gives you his Holy Spirit' so that you don't capitulate. It's not that you're not tempted. It's not that you're so floating above the earth. It's because God the Holy Spirit is in you calling you to walk with Jesus, to a pure and holy life, putting in godly discipline that takes you away from the edges where you know you're weak and unsafe. I remember coming back from a long run and feeling pretty tired. I jumped in the bath and there was the answer waiting to help me in my tiredness – Radox! It says, 'It will put new life into you.' What does the Spirit of God do? He puts new life into us.

As I close this evening, I want to just remind you of some very basic things. We all know we've got a long way to go. There are big areas where we've blown it. My second home when I was a child coming from Liverpool was a place called Drogheda, just about twenty-five or thirty miles up the coast of Dublin. The highest point in Drogheda is a place called Mill Mount and what was significant about Mill Mount, in this strong Catholic community, was at the very top was a cross. Not only was this cross at a high point, but it was an illuminated cross. It didn't matter wherever you went around Drogheda, however far you were away, when you looked up there was the cross. I always knew as a little kid that if I just walked in the direction of the cross I would find my way home. The way of the cross leads home. There the Lord Jesus lay down his life in sacrificial, substitutionary death so that I, the guilty one, may go free and I might receive the gift of his Spirit. Every time I slip and fail and wander away from him, I need to lift up my eyes and get back to that cross to find healing, forgiveness, grace and mercy and all that Christ has died to secure.

That is the gift of the Spirit. Do not quench the Spirit's fire, but rather be filled with the Spirit and go and live for Christ. So that whatever your circumstances, by the grace, you're enabled to sing in the rain.

Making Disciples of All Nations

by Jonathan Lamb

JONATHAN LAMB

Jonathan is currently the Director of Langham Preaching for Langham Partnership International, a mission working in fellowship with Christian leaders around the world which seeks to encourage a new generation of preachers and teachers. He has been chairman of the Keswick Convention and now serves as a Trustee and is also chairman of the Word Alive. Apart from teaching in a variety of contexts around the world, he is also a member of the preaching team in his local church, St Andrews, in Oxford. He is married to Margaret and they have three daughters.

Making Disciples of All Nations

Turn with me to Acts 20. We're going to look at verses 17-27.

Enchanted by the goal

Driving up to Keswick on Saturday, I enjoyed listening to a programme on the radio, called *Excess Baggage* and hosted by Sandy Toksvig. She was interviewing three mountaineers. She was trying to get at why they were willing to risk life and limb for climbing. After all, on Mount Blanc alone, the annual death toll is now in three figures. All of these mountaineers said they were 'enchanted by the goal'; by the summit, and the unspeakable beauty of the mountains which more than paid the cost they incurred. One of the mountaineers quoted the writing of another climber, called Herzog, who's written a book on his exploits. In fact, he had to dictate it because he lost all of his fingers from frostbite. This man said 'the summit was so much more important than fingers and toes.' It doesn't seem quite adequate to describe that as a hobby.

What are people living for?

As I listened to those people, I thought, 'Their lives are dominated by this all-consuming passion, this incredible sense of purpose.'

That stands in contrast to the way in which so many people live their lives today. If you ask people about their sense of purpose, what they give their life to. . . it's not that kind of passion and dedicated focused purpose. I read not long ago an answer to that question from Helena Bonham Carter, the actress, who I think sums up how many people, certainly in youth culture, view their lives. She said, 'We're going to die anyway, so what does it matter? So long as you have fun and have a sense of humour.' That's today's philosophy for many. It's 'eat, drink and watch telly, for tomorrow we diet.' That's the purpose of life. The purpose of life for so many of them is found in attributing meaning to things around them. It may be the things they consume, the things they wear, even the things they drive.

I was reading an article a short while ago on the crisis in the public sector. The journalist was talking about the way in which consumer culture has filled the vacuum left by the decline of traditional values, like patriotism, socialism or Christianity. He said: 'The most powerful collective identities now are those that we buy. So DKNY or CK mean more to your average teenager than any government service. Where once socialism offered the promise of a better world, now Gap does. Where once every seven-year-old girl wanted to be a teacher or a nurse, now they want to be Britney Spears. The consumer culture is primarily focused on your relationship with *yourself*, rather than a relationship with a wider cause. It's typified by the L'Oreal slogan, "Because you're worth it."'

You don't have to be a sophisticated social commentator to recognise that most people are looking for purpose, for meaning; something big to which they can give their lives. There frequently comes a point when people genuinely recognise that for all of their self-indulgence, all of their investment in those things, they remain deeply dissatisfied. They have no idea what should be the purpose of their existence.

What about your life? I'd like us all to confront that basic question, the question this text narrated, Acts 20. What are you giving your life to? What shapes your priorities? What determines your motivation?

Paul's purpose statement

Verse 24: 'I consider my life worth nothing to me, if only I may finish the race and complete the task the Lord Jesus has given me – the task of testifying to the gospel of God's grace.' See how Paul viewed his life. It wasn't a possession to be held onto at all costs. He wasn't living his life according to his *own* needs and priorities, his own sense of personal comfort, convenience or security. Here was a man with a purpose. His life was shaped by that one overriding concern which he expresses in verse 24, 'to be faithful to the Lord Jesus who called me to finish the task that God has given me.'

This speech is a wonderful example of what it means to make disciples. Although it's the task of the global Christian community to make disciples of all nations, it is essentially a calling for each individual Christian. I want to confront the personal demands involved in the global mission of God. Acts 20 is the only speech which Luke records which is addressed to a Christian audience. In particular it gives us unique insights into the pastoral and evangelistic priorities of Paul, and into what it took Paul to make disciples. I'd like us to look at four characteristics of Paul's ministry in making disciples of all nations. Each of these qualities is the result of that passionate purpose statement in verse 24, to 'complete the task the Lord Jesus has given me.'

Faithful proclamation

What comes across in this extraordinary commitment of Paul is his energetic commitment to preaching and teaching the gospel. Verse 24 – 'the task of testifying to the gospel of God's grace'. Verse 25 – 'I have gone about preaching the kingdom'. Verse 21, 'I have declared to both Jews and Greeks that they must turn to God in repentance and have faith in our Lord Jesus.' These are the great themes of the gospel that Paul is talking about: grace, faith, God's kingdom, human repentance. This speech demonstrates that Paul was thorough in fulfilling this aim of faithful proclamation of the gospel of God's grace.

To all the people

You can say it in three ways, this faithful proclamation. First it was to all of the people. Verse 21, 'I have declared to both Jews and Greeks that they must turn to God in repentance and have faith in our Lord Jesus.' In Acts 19, he was there in the city and teaching in the synagogue, arguing persuasively about the kingdom of God, and he had to move on. So he went to the lecture hall of Tyrannus. Acts 19:10, he lectured there for two years 'so that all the Jews and Greeks who lived in the province of Asia heard the word of the Lord.' It's a remarkable statement by Luke, '*all* the Jews and Greeks who lived in the province of Asia heard the word of the Lord' – all of the residents of Ephesus. It's been estimated that if Paul was there for about three years, and if he was in the lecture hall, say, five hours a day, then that is the equivalent to three forty-minute sermons a week for fifty years. That was his commitment to the preaching of that message. It was to *all* the people, literally making disciples of all nations in that cosmopolitan city.

All the truth

Notice in verse 27, '. . . I have not hesitated to proclaim to you the whole will of God.' His preaching ranged across every aspect of the plan and purpose of God. That's part of the business of making disciples. Every part of the message he proclaimed faithfully.

All occasions

That's another remarkable feature in this text that Luke gives us. He was equally thorough in his approach. Verse 20, 'You know that I have not hesitated to preach anything that would be helpful to you, but have taught you publicly and from house to house.' Verse 31: 'For three years I never stopped warning each of you night and day with tears.' This man wasted no opportunity. Nothing could stop Paul from this fundamental priority of the faithful proclamation of God's grace. No opposition, no trial, nothing could stop this man with a purpose. He omitted no part of the message, no part of the population, and no method was left untried. That's why in his speech, verse

26, he could be so bold in declaring, 'I am innocent of the blood of all men.' He's picking up the phrase which Ezekiel uses, Ezekiel 33, how he's fulfilled this task the Lord Jesus had given him. 'I've been a faithful watchman in my faithful proclamation of the gospel of God's grace.'

That's Paul's first priority, making disciples of all nations. I think it really does represent a challenge in terms of our own life and work, the work of the global church. What about all people? Are we tempted to ignore the difficult groups whether they're in our neighbourhoods, or in our society at large, or even other parts of the world? I often ask myself to what extent I am sustaining and developing this incredible vision of God's universal mission. That was the motivating force in Paul's life – *all* people to hear this gospel of God's grace. What about all of the truth? It's very tempting in our increasingly pluralistic culture to soft pedal parts of the message, which in our context are particularly difficult; for example, the uniqueness of Jesus Christ. Christians are losing their nerve about that part of the gospel in this pluralistic setting. Or the challenge of preaching repentance and faith. What about all occasions? I wonder if we're tempted to give up too easily. We assume it will never work. Paul would not give up. He was determined to hold nothing back, 'I have not hesitated to preach anything that would be helpful to you.'

Consistent living

Last month a small item of news that hit the international newspapers. A lorry driver had lost his job. He drove supply lorries for Coca-Cola, but he insisted on drinking Pepsi at work, so they sacked him. A little unjust, you might think. If it was the chief executive who was discovered with a six-pack of Pepsi under his desk, that would be another matter, because the new styles of business management all emphasise that consistency matters. Charles Handy, the business guru, lists as one of his six guiding principles for leaders and managers that the leader must live the vision. He must not only craft the mission statement for his company, he must embody it.

Verse 18, 'You know how I lived the whole time I was with you, from the first day I came into the province of Asia.' When you read this speech, there is a ring of integrity about it. 'This is the kind of person I am. You know this is how I lived among you.' The same is true of his closing words, verses 33–35. He says he has not coveted the possessions of others, he's worked hard, he's followed the words of the Lord Jesus, 'It is more blessed to give than to receive.' In other words, as you read through this text, you can see that he can appeal to them as witnesses of the way in which his life matched his words. This was and is an essential part of the task of making disciples. It's a reflection of the fundamental purpose of his calling. He was being true to that calling in verse 24, to proclaim faithfully and to live consistently.

In his most recent book, Dallas Willard tells the story of a pastor who one Sunday morning in the middle of the service saw something which made him very angry indeed. Immediately after the service he hunted out the person who was responsible for what happened and he gave him a ruthless, merciless rebuke. Unfortunately he was still wearing his lapel microphone. This was a large American church and his diatribe was broadcast right through the church buildings, in the Sunday school rooms, apparently even in the car park. Dallas Willard says soon afterwards he moved to another church.

I think almost all of us know that this is a fundamental challenge in Christian ministry of any kind – living by double standards. Paul's words in 1 Thessalonians echo exactly this same idea that is expressed here in verse 18 in talking to the Ephesian elders. Where he talks about his mission priorities he says, 'our gospel came not to you not simply with words but also with power, with the Holy Spirit and with deep conviction. You know how we lived among you for your sake.' Paul's description of mission in those opening verses in 1 Thessalonians 1 is a collection of items. It's not restricted to communicating information. That's not just the task of mission or of evangelism. He adds three other expressions in 1 Thessalonians 1:5: power, conviction, and in the Holy Spirit. But then there's a further phrase, which he gives in verse 5, and it's very tightly connected to everything else. He says, 'You know how we lived among you for your sake.' To the Thessalonians, as here to the believers in Ephesus he says, remember how we *lived*. The gospel that he was proclaiming was bearing fruit in his own life, and it was this combination which made his gospel communication so effective. God's word proclaimed in the power of the Spirit and demonstrated by being embodied in the messenger himself. This is to be expected because the truth of the gospel is dynamic. It is life-changing. Truth is to be *done*, not simply to be believed.

This kind of modelling of the gospel's faithful proclamation, and consistent living is vital today in whatever area of mission or ministry that God is calling us. Whatever our daily work, this combination is vital. Two of my teenage daughters over the last year or so have served on the staff of a theological college not far from where we live. They're cleaning the tables and serving up breakfast to the various ordinands and trainees at the theological college. Every so often, one of my daughters comes back Saturday afternoon and has another story to tell of how rude one or other of the students has been to her or to the girls who are serving the food or cleaning the tables. In fact, she's even threatened to e-mail the churches where these ordinands are going to go and give them an unsolicited testimonial about their ministry. On the one hand I say, 'We're all grumpy at breakfast, it's not too much.' But on the other, she is absolutely right. How do you make sense of less than godly behaviour of people who are preparing to serve the church, to make disciples? It's of vital importance in Christian mission that we ensure our lives are truly modelling the truth of the gospel, and that we're giving energy to the shaping and forming of other disciples through encouragement, through faithful proclamation, and through lives which demonstrate that kind of consistency.

If we're committed to the truth, it will shape the whole of our lives. Notice in the rest of the speech to the Ephesian elders, Paul takes this seriously. He says to the leaders, keep watch over yourselves. His first concern, you see, is that they take seriously their own lives. They pay attention to their own spiritual condition. Even though it's obvious, this is often missed. It's only as leaders themselves remain faithful to God as disciples that they can expect other people to do so. It's only as they grow in grace, in the knowledge of the Lord Jesus that they can appeal to others to do so, to move forward in faith. Yet so often this is a neglected priority amongst Christian workers, missionaries, pastors, all of us in whatever area of service God calls us to. We become spiritually dry with a busy schedule. We may even begin to drift morally or we are prone to a kind of professionalism, passing on information without any real connection to the spiritual life which should be maturing. Remember how Paul urged Timothy with exactly the same phrasing that he uses here in Acts 20, 'Don't let anyone look down on you because you are young, but set an example for the believers in speech, in life, in love, in faith and in purity. Watch your life and your doctrine closely, persevering in them, because if you do, you will save both yourself and your hearers.'

What is clear from this speech in Acts 20 is that there would be nothing in Paul's life, nothing in his lifestyle that could be made an excuse by other people for not believing in the gospel of God's grace. His message and his ministry were wedded to a godly life that made the message credible. That's essential to making disciples. That's the result of living with this kind of committed purpose.

Compassionate identification

This passage is wonderful for what it shows us about Paul's pastoral heart. He wasn't the professional who delivered his lectures and then disappeared. There is no hint here of a detached presence of a specialist. Let me highlight a few phrases. Verse 18: he lived amongst them for three years. Verse 19; he served the Lord with great humility and tears. Verse 20; he visited and taught from house to house; nothing remote in his engagement to people. Earlier on (which we didn't read) verses 9-11; he spent a very eventful night, proclaiming the word of the Lord, talking with the believers right through to daylight. At the end of chapter 20, you gain some insight into the affection that these believers held Paul in. Verse 37; 'They all wept as they embraced him and kissed him. What grieved them most was his statement that they would never see his face again.'

Here is someone who was completely open-hearted. He didn't keep his distance. He identified fully with the people to whom he was bringing this message, whom he was seeking to bring into true discipleship. As we've seen from that purpose statement, he didn't consider his own life, his own comforts, the first priority. He drew alongside people and in all kinds of costly ways he gave time and energy to understanding them and winning their trust and affection, just as he describes, again 1 Thessalonians, 'As apostles of Christ we could have been a burden to you, but we were gentle among you like a mother caring for her little children. We loved you so much that we were delighted to share with you not only the gospel of God but our lives as well, because you had become so dear to us.' Now there is probably no better description than that passage for what pastoral ministry, what making disciples involves; this unreserved commitment, sharing the gospel and our own lives. He worked hard to support himself, he constantly gave himself to others. The metaphor he uses here shows that deep love, that motherly gentleness.

As I think about the cause of the gospel around the world, I have no doubt at all that proclaiming the gospel is a very demanding task. But equally demanding is sharing our lives with those to whom we are bringing the message. Paul demonstrated that self-sacrifice that lies at the heart of this ministry of making disciples of all nations. This is simply following in the steps of Jesus himself. It's basic to this consistent service, sharing the gospel and ourselves with those to whom we are ministering. This is specially important in these days of postmodern culture. People are becoming weary of words. They do not trust authority figures any more. We don't trust the politicians, the BBC, church leaders. I was in a student residence not long ago. I went into the gentleman's bathroom and saw some words written above the hot air hand dryer: 'Press this button for a message from the Prime Minister.' People are cynical about words, weary of authority figures telling them what to do. We don't trust them any more. Authenticity in Christian mission demands our lives embody the message. We identify with those to whom the Lord is sending us. If the gospel describes God's power in the apparent weakness of Jesus, our ministry will follow that same pattern of costly identification. If God is calling you to go to another part of the world, I can guarantee it will involve that kind of costly identification if you are to make disciples of all nations.

Ajith Fernando has written a book recently called *Jesus Driven Ministry*, in which he says a lot about identification and a lot to us comfortable western Christians, as he would call us. He highlights the fact that many people are not prepared for the costs of this kind of mission, this kind of disciple-making. We are more concerned with self-fulfilment than with the costly identification with others. We're more interested in the 'because you're worth it' mentality. When you are committed to the gospel and you live with *that* mentality you will soon be disillusioned in your service. If God is calling you to serve him in mission it's as well to be realistic about what Paul is saying. He shows his humility, he refuses to claim anything for himself. He talks about his tears, his deep concern for his converts, he displays patience and perseverance as he keeps going year after year, proclaiming the word, refusing to give in. In my work with younger pastors and leaders I sometimes quote the words of Colin Morris in talking about preaching. He says it's not from a pulpit but from a cross that power-filled words are spoken. Sermons need to be seen as well as heard to be effective. Eloquence, homiletical skills, biblical knowledge are not enough. Anguish, pain, engagement, sweat and blood puncture the stated truths to which men will listen.

Obedient suffering

Paul describes, in verse 22 onwards, what he expects will now face him as he carries to fulfilment this task that the Lord Jesus has given him. It was uncertain what his future held. 'I am going to Jerusalem, not knowing what will happen to me there.' He knew it would involve suffering. Verse 23, 'in every city the Holy Spirit warns me that prison and hardships are facing me.' It was an uncertain future, but it was necessary. Verse 22, he says, '. . . compelled by the Spirit, I am . . .' Several times he talks about this kind of compulsion. Despite the warnings of what he would encounter, he knew that God was calling him to go, the Spirit was pushing him forward so he must obey.

A short while ago there was a report in the *British Journal of General Practice* which carried a survey of the stresses and strains on British missionaries. *The Times'* medical correspondent reported on this article. This is what he said: 'One hundred years after David Livingstone died, broken by disease and despair in a remote African village, British missionaries are afflicted by the same occupational hazards that hastened his demise.' He went on to describe this survey. Two hundred missionaries were surveyed and a high proportion of those were brought home for health reasons; 60 per cent had psychiatric illness of one kind or another. Livingstone himself was found dead kneeling in prayer beside his bed, on May 1st 1873 in what is now called Zambia. *The Times'* correspondent continued, 'by the time Stanley found him, he was worn out mentally and physically, his supplies had been stolen, he had no medicines, he was almost at the end of the road.'

When you read Acts 20, you realise Paul already knew a great deal about the costs of making disciples. He refers in verse 3 to the plots of the Jews. He had to make other plans because of the plots of the Jews. And then again in a poignant phrase in verse 19 of the passage we are looking at, 'I served the Lord with great humility and with tears, although I was severely tested by the plots of the Jews.' Like Jesus who called him, if obedience required it, then he was willing to suffer. I think that's the only way that you can make sense of these two apparently contradictory messages of the Spirit in verses 22, 23. Verse 22, it's a compulsion by the Spirit that drives him to Jerusalem; and in verse 23, the warning that he will suffer if he goes to Jerusalem. How is that contradiction reconciled? It's reconciled by the purpose statement that we've been looking at in verse 24: 'I consider my life worth nothing to me if only I may finish the race and complete the task the Lord Jesus has given me'. Obedient suffering was no problem to a man who understood his life in those terms – Jesus calling me. That's an expression of these four qualities that we've identified; faithful proclamation, consistent living, compassionate identification, obedient suffering. I think those four things are all needed if we are going to make disciples of all nations. Verse 24 is a call for total commitment. We have seen what this meant for Paul. He gave everything he had to make disciples. He wanted to finish that task.

I have an inspirational poster at home which brings me great encouragement. It says this, 'God put me on earth to accomplish a certain number of things. Right now I am so far behind I will never die.' Paul expresses in this purpose statement what he also wrote to Timothy. He was determined to finish the course. 'I have fought the good fight, I have finished the race, I have kept the faith.' He completed the task the Lord Jesus had given. He had made disciples of all nations. He had lived his life with that kind of undivided purpose. It's worth it for that overwhelming beauty of Jesus and the call of Jesus; to proclaim the gospel of God's grace.

I have, over the years, received news from my brothers and sisters in Rwanda and Burundi. Not all of the Christians in those countries capitulated to racism or to ethnic hatred. Some of them opposed it and often at the cost of their lives, and in the midst of genocide, stood for Christian gospel principles of forgiveness and reconciliation. One of my former colleagues whose life was preserved in the middle of it was left there with his wife and family in the refugee camps. A number of us found some money, sent him a fax and said we can fly you out, we can get your family out. He replied with this very short fax, 'If I cannot share my people's pain, I cannot share the gospel with them.' There's nothing half-hearted or double-minded about that reply. Here was someone like Paul, whose focus was sharp, whose purpose was absolutely clear. He knew why he was living his life. So it was for Paul. His life was of no value to him, he said. He was ready to lay it down. His ambition was not to climb some ecclesiastical ladder, but to finish the race, to complete the task of proclaiming the gospel. He wasn't after fame or money. He was absolutely focused on this task of making disciples, of proclaiming the good news.

I ask if God is calling you to that task. The calling to serve God in bringing the good news to the nations is not driven by self-fulfilment, but by the calling of Jesus Christ himself. This text shows there are no false promises, no immediate rewards, save knowing that we serve the Lord Christ, that we fulfil the task he has given us, that we run that race, that we climb to the summit. Because to be a disciple of Jesus is simply this: to take up our cross and to follow him. That's it, pure and simple. Verse 24: 'I consider my life worth nothing to me, if only I may finish the race and complete the task the Lord Jesus has given me — the task of testifying to the gospel of God's grace.'

Just Like Jesus

by Dave Richards

DAVE RICHARDS

Converted at the age of seventeen through Altrincham Baptist Church in Cheshire. Dave worked for UCCF for three years, leading numerous university missions before working as an evangelist for St Johns, Harborne, Birmingham. He then become curate at Knowle parish church, Solihull, before moving to Edinburgh to lead a large, city- centre evangelical church at St Paul's and St George's Scottish Episcopal Church as their Rector. He also leads a monthly seeker-event called 'icon'. He is very keen on sport and supports Manchester United. He loves good holidays and nice wine! His wife Cathy is a consultant clinical psychologist and they have three young children.

Just like Jesus

Introduction

How many of you are on holiday? Isn't it the way that when you are away from work, away from home, God somehow sneakily will say things to you, and you're in a position where you can hear them? Four years ago I was on holiday in America. Some friends were working over in the States and they said 'We'd love to pay for you to come as a family and spend three weeks with us in America.' That is not the sort of offer you turn down, so we said 'Yes, we're coming.' Because I had young kids, I hadn't taken many books with me to read on holiday. Before I had kids, I used to take loads of books, but young children sort of preclude reading on holiday. So the friend that we were staying with said 'I've got some books on the bookshelf, pick one out and have a read.' She came back about an hour later, and I was on page 3. She looked at me and said 'You're quite a slow reader' and I said to her 'I don't actually feel that I need to read any more.' Because God had taken that opportunity to speak to me in a very clear and direct way. The book that I picked up was *Just Like Jesus* by Max Lucado. In his opening chapter he writes these words

> What if, for one day, Jesus were to become you? What if, for twenty-four hours, Jesus wakes up in your bed, walks in your shoes, lives in

your house, assumes your schedule? Your boss becomes his boss, your mother becomes his mother, your pains become his pains? With one exception, nothing about your life changes. Your health doesn't change. Your circumstances don't change. Your schedule isn't altered. Your problems aren't solved. Only one change occurs.

What if, for one day and one night, Jesus lives your life with his heart? Your heart gets the day off, and your life is led by the heart of Christ. His priorities govern your actions. His passions drive your decisions. His love directs your behaviour.

What would you be like? Would people notice a change? Your family – would they see something new? Your co-workers – would they sense a difference? What about the less fortunate? Would you treat them the same? And your friends? Would they detect more joy? How about your enemies? Would they receive more mercy from Christ's heart than from yours?

And you? How would you feel? What alterations would this transplant have on your stress level? Your mood swings? Your temper? Would you sleep better? Would you see sunsets differently? Death differently? Taxes differently? Any chance you'd need fewer aspirins? How about your reaction to traffic delays? Would you still dread what you are dreading? Better yet, would you still do what you are doing?

Would you still do what you had planned to do for the next twenty-four hours? Obligations. Engagements. Outings. Appointments. With Jesus taking over your heart, would anything change?

Keeping working on this for a moment. Adjust the lens of your imagination until you have a clear picture of Jesus leading your life, then snap the shutter and frame the image. What you see is what God wants. He wants you to 'think and act like Christ Jesus' (Phil. 2:5).

God's plan for you is nothing short of a new heart. If you were a car, God would want control of your engine. If you were a computer, God would claim the software and the hard drive. If you were an aeroplane, he'd take his seat in the cockpit. But you are a person, so God wants to change your heart. God wants you to be just like Jesus. God loves you just the way you are, but he refuses to leave you that way. He wants you to be just like Jesus.[1]

I was deeply challenged by those words. I'd been a Christian over twenty years. I'd been in the ministry a few, and yet with lightning clarity I saw that what God wanted for my life, and for each and every one of us who belongs to Jesus, is that throughout the course of our lives we become like Jesus. So the things that we say, the way in which we react, are the things that Jesus would want to do if he lived in our place. In Philippians chapter 1:6, Paul says that we have been inaugurated into Christ. He says I thank my God for all of you, 'being confident of this, that he who began a good work in you will carry it on to completion until the day of Christ Jesus.' When we became a Christian God began a good work in each and every single one of us. He inaugurated us into Christ. But he doesn't want to leave us there.

There is nothing that we can do that will make God love us more than he already loves us. He simply loves us, not because of anything that we have done. In fact despite the things that we do, and despite the people that we are, God simply loves us. Nothing that we can do, no matter how long we've been a Christian, will make God love us more. He loves us just the way we are. He accepts us like that. But he wants us to become more like Jesus. He is putting, as it were, the finishing touches to our lives. Some of us need more finishing touches than others, but that is God's aim, for you and me to become like Jesus.

Be Christ-centred

As a church, we were going through a process of adopting a mission statement and discerning about ten values that made us distinctive as

---

[1] Lucado, Max, *Just Like Jesus* (Nashville: Thomas Nelson, 1998)

a church. It was a very useful exercise and we come back to it every eighteen months or so and say 'What is it that we exist for as a church? What is it that God is calling us to do as St Paul's and St George's?' We decided that value number one should be this:'We believe that we should be Christ-centred in all we do. Our aim as a church is to point people to Jesus and to worship him with all of our lives. We want to become like Jesus.' That value determines the way in which we as a church spend our money. It determines who we employ, the activities that we do and the activities that we don't do. And what's true for a church should also be true of us as individuals; we should aim to become like Jesus.

In Paul's letter to the Philippians in chapter 2 we have this stated very clearly. Paul's letter to the church at Philippi is essentially a thank you letter for a financial gift that he had received from this church. This letter was written by Paul, probably in about AD61 while he was under house arrest. It was a church very close to Paul's heart. He helped to plant this church, probably in about AD50. Philippi was a city in north-east Greece. It had no Jewish synagogue but instead a small, faithful, Jewish community used to meet by the river to pray on the Sabbath. There Paul met Lydia, a God-fearer, a non-Jew, a business woman who traded textiles. She'd become a Christian and the Philippian church had been born.

There's something else that we need to know about the city of Philippi. Philippi was a place where people were quite proud to live. It was one of the addresses to have in the Roman Empire. If you said that you came from Philippi, you would get more respect. To be a citizen of Philippi, because it was a Roman colony, was to be the equivalent of a citizen of Rome. The people in Philippi began to wear Roman clothes, to speak Latin, observe Roman customs and build using Roman architecture. Also, Philippi was a city full of ex-soldiers, legionaries and centurions. Think of a place where ex-military people go to live. If you're from the south coast of England, it might be Eastbourne or Tunbridge Wells. It was a great city and had a great church, that was very close to Paul's heart.

Disunity

There was a problem, and the problem in the church at Philippi was one that afflicts many, many churches. It was disunity. Disunity is a killer; it can wreck a sports team, split a political party and immobilise a church. Just two weeks ago I was speaking to somebody (they don't come to my church). We were talking about their church and how they felt towards their church. They just poured out their heart as to how unhappy they felt in this church, and how they didn't feel the teaching was helpful to them, but they stuck in there. After a while I asked them a few questions. 'Have you ever spoken of your concern, of your frustration, of your unhappiness with the leader of your church?' 'No, I've never done that.' 'How do you think they would feel if they knew how unhappy you were in their church?' 'Don't know.' 'Don't you think you should go and talk to them about your unhappiness?' 'Maybe.' I said 'What sort of God would want you to stay if you were that unhappy?' They promised to think it through. There are people who come to St Paul's and St George's Church, who are unhappy in my church. I would love that they could be happy but I would far rather they found another church where they could serve, grow, and feel they belonged.

These former soldiers in Philippi, ironically, knew the power and effect of unity. The Roman army was famous for its massed ranks and winning formations. They would get all the soldiers together and their shields were designed to fit together. There were classic tactics like the tortoise and the wall, and they would overwhelm the opposition because they would stay together. That's the imagery that Paul is using at the end of chapter 1, verses 27 and 28. He says 'Contend as one man for the faith of the gospel. Stand firm in the Spirit.' That would have triggered immediate pictures for these ex-military types who knew what it was to stand together.

But their church was wracked by disunity and so Paul gives them three reasons to be united. Firstly in chapter 2 and verses 1 and 2 he says 'If you have any encouragement from being united in Christ . . .' Literally, what he is saying is 'Has Jesus ever come and whispered in your ear?' There's been a time when you have felt far away from

God. There's been a time maybe when, either in a hospital ward, or in a consulting room, or by the side of a road accident, or on the end of a telephone line, you've been tempted to give up on the Christian faith. And at the time when you need God most, he's come and just whispered words of encouragement in your ear, and those simple few words of encouragement have been enough to keep you going. Has Jesus ever come and whispered words of encouragement in your ear?

How's your heart?

Secondly, have you received comfort from his love? Has God's love helped you in your darkest moments? When all else seemed to vanish and you were left simply alone, has God's love ever reached out to you in those worst of times?

Thirdly, have you any fellowship with the Holy Spirit? Literally, have you ever taken a handful of God's Spirit? Have you ever felt that refreshing Spirit pour into your life? And fourthly, have you any tenderness or compassion? Literally again, has your heart been melted, making you more aware of other people and their needs? Has God's tenderness, love and compassion towards you changed your heart? As one speaker says 'Is your heart getting bigger for God and people, or is your heart getting smaller for God and people?'

Paul says, if the answer is 'yes' to these four questions then this is how you should live. If the answer is 'yes' verse 2 'make my joy complete ...' Remember where Paul is. He's under house arrest. How was his joy going to be made complete? By the Philippian Christians staging a rescue mission to spring him from prison? By him being sent a food parcel by them? He says 'Be like-minded'. Be one in spirit, heart and purpose. What he isn't appealing for is uniformity. We have this idea that we're all to become like Jesus, that we're all simply to become clones. Is your picture of heaven a place where everybody is the same? Heaven will not be like that because the paradox is that as you and I become more like Jesus, we become more like the people we were always intended to be. We become who God made us to be and always inten-ded us to be. We won't become all the same. What Paul is appealing for here is not uniformity but unity, and the two are very different things.

Look at other people

How does that happen? Paul, in verses 3 and 4, says 'Look at other people.' In the ancient world humility was considered a vice. It had connotations of being weak. It wasn't the sort of argument that would have been your first choice to appeal to a group of ex-soldiers. Yet this is the basis of Paul's appeal. Verse 3 'Do nothing out of selfish ambition or vain conceit, but in humility consider others better than yourselves.' You want to know how to become like Jesus, how this works in practice? You look to other people and you consider them better than yourselves. For many, many years I've been a supporter of Manchester United. Sir Alex Ferguson says that it took him about five years of being the manager of Manchester United before he could say to his team 'Look around the dressing room, and as you look around the dressing room be able to say "I'm glad he's in my team and not the opposition because he's the best in his position."' I wonder if you're in a church leadership team, if you could look on the people on your PCC, in your diaconate, whatever church you belong to, and you'd be able to say of them 'I'm so glad they're on my team and they're not in the opposition's.' By that I don't mean the church down the road. But you are really pleased that they're on your team, because you can't think of anybody that you would rather have. As you think of your church leadership meeting, however it functions, you look forward to those meetings if you're on that body, or you pray for that body, because you know the right people are in the right positions. This is the basis of Paul's appeal.

Verse 4: think again who he was writing this to. This doesn't come naturally to your average retired army colonel. If we're honest we will always have mixed motives, but how much of what we do, at work, in the home, and especially sometimes in the church, is motivated by how it will make us look in the eyes of other people? About what other people will think of us, rather than what God thinks of us?

Look to Jesus

Why does Paul make this appeal? Well, thirdly, and finally, he says in verse 5 to 11, in this amazing hymn, 'Look to Jesus.' For many years when I worked in Edinburgh we had Richard Holloway as our Bishop. He was actually always extremely supportive of St Paul's and St George's and as a Bishop was pastorally superb. He said this about Jesus. 'The source of all power limits that power in himself, and empties himself of it.' These verses, 6 to 11, are perhaps the highest Christology in the New Testament, written within twenty years of the resurrection. For years I misread verse 6. I think probably that some time in the past I actually read a translation, which was a mistranslation. Many of us you see read it this way. 'Your attitude should be the same as that of Christ Jesus: Who though being in very nature God.' It doesn't actually say that. Not 'though being in very nature God'. It's 'because he was in nature God'. It's almost as if Jesus can't help himself. He's reflecting the character of the Godhead. And the God who we believe in and the God we worship is a God who does things like this. It's part of God's nature to serve, to defer.

Jesus empties himself because he can't help himself. The technical word is *kenosis*; it means, literally, empty himself. And that's what Jesus did. Not of his deity, but he emptied himself of his rank. He emptied himself of his rights, his privilege, his glory, all his divine prerogatives. He invented downward mobility. Human, slave, death, death on a cross. It doesn't come much lower than that. Naked, humiliated, crucified, the servant king. He was dying in our place so that we might be forgiven, but he was also laying a pattern down for you and for me. You want to know how to become like Jesus, then look at Philippians chapter 2 verses 6 to 11. You think you've got rights, privileges, status? Look at Jesus, and what he did with that; not following the world's expectation of status, power, achievement or recognition, but emptying himself. You need to go down before you can go up. For you and for me it will mean different things. It will mean emptying ourselves of our pride, our ego, our jealousy, our greed, our selfish nature, our ambition. Emptying ourselves of envy, false modesty, judgementalism, vanity. To each of us it will have different implications.

The power. . .

Paul is utterly realistic. Look across to chapter 3, verses 10 to 11. He says 'I want to know Christ'. Not 'more about Christ', I want to deepen my relationship with him and know him better. How does that happen? Through two things happening, says Paul; knowing his power and sharing his sufferings. That's the paradox at the heart of the Christian faith, power and sufferings. Power. That same power that raised Christ from the dead is at work in you and me. Jesus did not rise from the dead. Jesus was raised from the dead. There's all the difference, in this world and the next. When Jesus was dead he was dead. There was nothing he could do. But then God's Spirit came afresh into him and he was raised again to new life. Paul says that that same power, that same *dunamis*, that same dynamite that raised Jesus Christ from the dead is at work in you and me. That same power. All the resources of heaven are available for you and for me.

Gordon Fee, an amazing charismatic academic theologian, says this 'Paul is no triumphalist, all glory without pain. But neither does he know anything of the gloomy stoicism that's often exhibited in historic Christianity, where the life of the believer is to basically slug it out in the trenches with little or no sense of Christ's presence or power.' That may well be how you've come to this week. You're just slugging it out as a Christian. God seems miles away. You almost don't know why you've come. God's presence and power seem miles away.

. . .and the suffering

But it's not just the power, it's also about sharing in his suffering. As we become more like Jesus we will know pain, it's part of being a Christian. Many writers, many theologians, many church leaders, many preachers will want to bypass this point. You cannot bypass it because it's there in Scripture. It's the paradox at the heart of the Christian faith. Power, but also pain. As we 'know Christ and the power of his resurrection, and the fellowship of sharing in his sufferings, becoming like him in his death, and so, somehow, to attain the resurrection from the dead', we become like Jesus. The problem in many of our churches is that we know people who've been in those churches for years. Some are young, some old, some young and cranky and some old and cranky. We think that they need to change. The bad news is there are people looking at us thinking the same thing. Change is part of being a Christian. God loves us just the way we are, but he loves us too much to leave us that way. His aim is for you and for me to become more like Jesus. That every year, we should be becoming more like Christ.

C.S. Lewis said this. 'Our faith is not a matter of hearing what Christ said long ago and trying to carry it out. Rather the real Son of God is at your side, and he is beginning to turn you into the same kind of thing as himself. He is beginning, so to speak to inject his kind of life, and thought, his *zoe*, his life into you. Beginning to turn a tin soldier into a live human being. And the part of you that doesn't like it is the part that's still tin.' For different ones of us that tin will be different things. But if we're honest before God, it may well be that we know the things that are resisting the Spirit of God. We are resisting becoming more like Jesus in some character trait, in some habit and we know it's not the way Jesus would behave or react, but we've done it for years. It may be something that we think we've hidden from God. We've hidden it from other people, at times maybe when we've hidden it perhaps even from ourselves and, bizarrely, at times we think that we've hidden it from God. God graciously and lovingly is waiting for us to bring it out into the open and to confess what it is, to give it to him and to say 'Lord, please make me more like Jesus.'

Pitfalls and Hazards in Discipleship III

by John Risbridger

JOHN RISBRIDGER

Growing up in a Christian home, John grew into an active faith at a young age and his mid teens and student years were a time of particular growth. He joined UCCF in 1994 after five years in hospital management. For six years he led the Southern team of UCCF staff and volunteer workers before taking over the role of Head of Student Ministries in September 2000. John serves as a Trustee of the Keswick Convention and is as excited as ever about the opportunities for the gospel among students. John is married to Alison and they have two daughters. He loves hill walking and squash but his favourite pastime is lying on the floor listening to John Rutter's music!

JOHN KIMBALL

Pitfalls and Hazards

Introduction

A while back I was sat on platform number 2 of our local railway station, waiting for a delayed train to Cheltenham. I travel a lot by train and I have found that time waiting for delayed trains is great time to pray. As a result, my prayer life has blossomed over the last few years because I have travelled on a lot of trains. That particular Wednesday morning I was quietly praying away about some of the challenges of the day, feeling some of the weakness I often feel at the start of a new day. I found myself saying, 'Lord if only I was more godly... please will you make me more holy?' Almost immediately the question popped into my head, 'Do you want to be more godly?' 'Of course I do,' I replied. The question came straight back. 'No, do you *really* want to be more godly?' As I thought about that question for a few minutes, I had to face the fact that there were actually a whole range of voices in my heart wanting all kinds of different things. I want to be more godly, but I also want to be able to hold onto a little bit of busyness here and there, spread a little bit of gossip, keep my standard of living the same and not get myself involved in anything that might get a bit messy. As I thought, my mind went back to a sermon I'd heard years before where someone had said 'You are as holy as you want to be.' I wasn't sure I completely agreed with that at the time, but it was very challenging, because it made me face the ambiguity that was there within my own heart. In his own inimitable way, Woody Allen once commented, 'The only thing standing between me and greatness, is me.'

Double-mindedness

Isn't it sometimes the case that for us in our Christian lives the thing that stands between me and authentic Christian discipleship is actually *me*? I want God, but I want him on my terms. Yes, I want to grow, but I want to be able to set the price of my growth. I want to be close to God, but I want to be able to keep my space from him in areas of my life where his presence might become uncomfortable. I'm the biggest obstacle in my growth of Christian discipleship. You know that kind of thinking that says, 'I want God, but on my terms,' that kind of thinking is what the Bible sometimes describes as 'double-mindedness.' I want to suggest to you that it's exactly that kind of double-mindedness that lies at the heart of many of the pitfalls and the hazards that we face in our Christian discipleship.

Earlier we saw how hazardous serious mountain climbing can be. But the biggest challenges are not in the conditions on the mountain, but in the heart and the mind of the mountaineer. Sir Edmund Hillary, who first conquered Everest back in 1953, put it like this, 'It's not the mountain we conquer, it's ourselves.' I think motivation is the single most important factor in any sort of success. A basic motivation, the desire to succeed, to stretch yourself to the utmost is the most important factor. It's precisely at the level of motivation that double-mindedness kicks in and undermines our Christian discipleship. I suspect that the tendency to double-mindedness is particularly strong amongst us Christians in the west today. We live in a culture where faith is seen simply as a lifestyle choice, where church is a leisure activity and where deep commitment is in short supply. We always want to make sure that we keep our options open. In such a world, double-mindedness thrives, weakening our resolve, leaving us off-guard, prone to temptation, easy prey, ready to fall into the next pitfall that comes our way. I want to explore this problem of double-mindedness in three short passages. The first one is at the end of Luke 9:57.

Will you follow me wherever. . . ?

'As they were walking along the road, a man said to him, "I will follow you wherever you go."'. Put yourself in Jesus' position. What are
you going to do when someone comes up to you and says, 'I want to
follow Jesus now. Please.' You say, 'You want to follow Jesus right now?
Here's the prayer. Come on, say the prayer, get into the kingdom now,
quickly.' It's what we do, isn't it? Or if we didn't have quite the courage
we'd say 'We're running an Enquirers group at our church, why don't
you come along?' But Jesus' response is so different.

Verse 58: 'Jesus replied, "Foxes have holes and birds of the air have
nests, but the Son of Man has nowhere to lay his head."' Jesus isn't
saying that all true Christians must sleep rough. But if we follow him
there are no guarantees of earthly security. He's testing the double-
mindedness in this man's claim to commitment. 'Do you *really* mean
you want to follow wherever I go? That could cost you.' Jesus tests
this man's commitment. He wants to root out the double-mindedness, to press him for his bottom line. Is it following Jesus, or about
being comfortable? Most of us, most of the time, do have somewhere to lay our heads. Jesus isn't saying that's wrong. But isn't it the
case that we do still face moments of critical decision where our
bottom line gets exposed? Is it following Jesus or is it being comfortable? Maybe it's a challenge to sacrificial giving. Maybe it's a
decision to give up our homes and security and serve God in another culture in another part of the world. Maybe it's a decision to
take a stand in the workplace on some issue of principle knowing
that that may cost you a great deal, even your job, certainly promo-
tion. In those critical moments when the chips are down, Jesus is
saying, what comes first? What's the bottom line? Is it following
Jesus, or is it our comfort?

Will you follow me now?

Next, Jesus calls a man to follow him. It's the other way around this
time. The man's response again reveals his double-mindedness straight

away. Verse 59: 'He said to another man, "Follow me." But the man replied, "Lord first let me go and bury my father."' It seems a reasonable enough request, doesn't it? Think about it. If this man's father has just died, and they haven't even had the funeral, what's he doing coming to Jesus talking about being his disciple? Surely he's got family business to undertake. What's probably going on here is that this fellow's father is still alive and the man is using his family responsibilities as an excuse to postpone serious commitment. He's saying, 'I will follow you when it's convenient to me. When I've sorted out some of the most important things in my life, when it suits my circumstances.' That's double-mindedness in commitment. That's what draws the sharpness of Jesus' response. Verse 60: 'Jesus said to him, "Let the dead bury their own dead, but you go and proclaim the kingdom of God."'

The truth is that following Jesus and taking our discipleship seriously is rarely convenient.

'Lord, when I've finished my studies, then I'll start being really serious about my faith and get involved in evangelism. You've got to understand there are finals coming.'

'Lord, I'm just starting in my career now. Things are really a bit tight at the moment, just taken on a mortgage. Lord, just a couple of years, then I'll get involved properly in a church somewhere. It's just not the time at the moment.'

'Lord it's really tough bringing up a family, you know. I've never been so tired. I keep going to sleep when I'm praying because I'm tired because I've been up half the night with the kids. When the kids have grown up, then I'll take my discipleship seriously.'

'Lord, it's so peaceful now that the kids have left home at last. At last I can enjoy the fruit of all these years of work. Surely you wouldn't want to deny a man the opportunity to just have a few years to have a good time in the prime of his life, would you?'

'Lord, I've retired and my health is beginning to fail me. I'm slowing down a bit. I'm not really sure that I've got too much left to give you.'

Following Jesus is rarely convenient. It rarely fits in with our circumstances. Of course, there are different seasons of life, each with their own constraints and their own possibilities. That's just reality.

But the priority is still always the same: verse 60: '. . . you go and proclaim the kingdom of God.'

Will you follow me only?

Again it seems a reasonable request: 'Another one said, "I will follow you, Lord, but first let me go back and say goodbye to my family"' (v61). It seems perfectly reasonable. But Jesus sees through what the man is saying. He's wavering. He's felt the impact of what Jesus has said and half of him wants to go with it, but the cost seems too high. He wants to go home, maybe to escape the discomfort of continuing to face the challenge of Jesus' presence. Or maybe he wants to keep a foot in both camps. Jesus replies with a classic image which expresses the heart of double-mindedness. Verse 62: Jesus says, 'No-one who puts his hand to the plough and looks back is fit for service in the kingdom of God.' How on earth could you plough a straight furrow if you're looking in the opposite direction? It would be completely impossible. It's the classic picture of double-mindedness, trying to plough while looking backwards. Kidding yourself that you're doing the work of the kingdom when actually all your attention and all your priorities are focused on maintaining the lifestyle that you've always had.

Isn't it the case that as we see Jesus exposing the double-mindedness of these three would-be disciples that we find him exposing our double-mindedness too? Certainly that's what happens to me when I read this passage. We say we're committed to Christ, but there are other voices too. Voices just like the voices we've read of in Luke 9 here. Voices that are seeking comfort, convenience; voices pressing us to keep a foot in both camps. We're double-minded in our basic commitment to Jesus Christ. If we let those voices begin to set the agenda for us in our lives, we'll soon find ourselves walking down a road full of many pitfalls and hazards. Jesus presses us for *our* bottom line. He challenges *us* to clear, unequivocal, single-minded commitment to Christ. Where is the rub for you? Where is the challenge? What is it that the Lord is asking you to let go of? Where is it that *your* commitment to Christ has become compromised?

Double-mindedness in what we love

If you just turn over to 1 John 2, I want us to explore double-mindedness in what we love.

> Do not love the world or anything in the world. If anyone loves the world, the love of the Father is not in him. For everything in the world – the cravings of sinful man, the lust of his eyes and the boasting of what he has and does – comes not from the Father but from the world. The world and its desires pass away, but the man who does the will of God lives for ever (1 Jn. 2:15–17).

We were reminded in the Bible reading this morning about the desperate consequences of double-mindedness in a marriage. But as Hosea's story was beginning to suggest, we can find ourselves as Christians taking on divided loyalties in our relationship with God. To challenge our double-mindedness, John faces us with a stark choice as to what we love. He says there's a choice between the love of the world and the love of the Father. Verse 15: 'Do not love the world or anything in the world. If anyone loves the world, the love of the Father is not in him.'

What does John mean exactly by loving the world? John uses this word 'the world' in a rather particular way. He usually uses it to refer to human life lived without reference to God, or even human life in active rebellion against God. An attitude that sees God as completely irrelevant and on the fringes of our thinking, if he's there at all. We had that great example of Alastair Campbell saying 'We don't do God around here.' There was a similar thing when Tony Blair was asked to whom he ultimately felt accountable for taking the decision he had taken to go to war. He said ultimately he was responsible to his Creator. You may have read some of the response that provoked in the press afterwards. That whole idea that it is just completely irrelevant to think about our accountability to God. That's the essence of worldliness, according to John. John is saying, 'You can't claim to love God and love the world. It doesn't make sense. You can't claim that you love God and then live like everybody else as if God weren't relevant at all. It doesn't make sense!'

Unbridled desires

He points out the contrast for us in two specific ways. First of all in verse 16 he says the world is driven by unbridled desires. John describes the way the world functions. He says everything in the world, 'the cravings of sinful man, the lust of his eyes and the boasting of what he has and does – these things come not from the Father but from the world.' Worldliness, being worldly, isn't primarily about the clothes you choose to wear or the music you choose to listen to or exactly how you spend your social time. The essence of worldliness is about what drives you, about what you love and value. Are you driven by these instincts for fame, sex, money, power? Or are you driven by the desire to do the will of God and to live for his pleasure? That's the choice that John puts before us and it goes right to our hearts, to what we actually love. Is it satisfying our appetites, or is it seeking the pleasure of God? What's the bottom line for us? We see it all around in society. I see it, I want it, I must have it, I deserve it. So go and get it. Lust and craving which must be instantly fulfilled. That's the heart of worldliness.

Focus on eternity

John says, it's not appropriate for those who claim to love the Father. These two loves are incompatible. Then the second difference comes where he says, 'The world and its desires pass away, but the man who does the will of God lives for ever (v17). So the second choice: the world focuses on the here and now, but those who love God focus on eternity. Stand in the middle of a busy city during rush hour and just watch what's going on. Allow it to impact on you; the sadness of the whole situation. It's so ridiculous when you stop and think, isn't it? Everybody's spending all their time, often ruining themselves, ruining their health, ruining their families to get things that they won't be able to take with them when they die. Don't you ever ask yourself what's the point?

Don't misunderstand me, work is very important. It's part of God's gift to us in creation that we are to work. But this drivenness to possess more and more doesn't make sense. The gospel subverts all of that. The gospel shows us a bigger vision, that there is more to life than just obeying your thirst. We *can* invest our lives in something that will last for ever, we *can* give ourselves for the fulfilment of God's eternal purposes. We can live our lives for him, now, and we can share eternity with him. That's the perspective of those who love the Father. They're wanting to invest their lives in things that will last for ever.

Are you in love with the world? Are you allowing yourself to be driven by the desire for pleasure, wealth or fame? Or are you in love with the Father? Longing to please him, to fulfil his purposes for your life? How many times have we seen people make shipwreck of their faith because they have allowed themselves to start loving the world. They began to think that they had the right to satisfy their sexual desires in an ungodly way. That they had the right to satisfy the demands of their ego, the right to a lifestyle that was just one or two notches further up the ladder from where they were. They began to love the world and the love of the Father was squeezed out and their discipleship ended up nowhere. These are the pitfalls that face us today in the western world.

Double-mindedness in facing hardship

Flick back to James 1. I'm very conscious in a group this size there'll be many people who are going through hard times and for whom I may touch a few raw nerves. I pray that God will give me grace to speak with gentleness and understanding. It's interesting, though, that James himself appears to have no such worries as he addresses a church that's suffering and scattered. James 1:2, he comes straight out with it: 'Consider it pure joy, my brothers, whenever you face trials of many kinds'. How can there possibly be pure joy in all these trials of many kinds? It seems ridiculous. It seems hopelessly, pastorally insensitive for James to say that. But you see, James is challenging the way that we often think about suffering and hardship. His answer is that hardship is fundamentally about testing. Hardship *is* testing and such testing is so significant an instrument in the hands of God that it will lead us to maturity so that in eternal terms we lack nothing.

Just follow the argument through. Verses 2-4: 'Consider it pure joy, my brothers, whenever you face trials of many kinds, because you know that the testing of your faith develops perseverance. Perseverance must finish its work so that you may be mature and complete, not lacking anything.' This is an incredibly radical perspective on hardship in our lives. We always feel that when we face hardship, that hardship will impoverish us. It somehow makes us poorer. But James says, think about it differently. There is another perspective, he says. In such times God wants to give us things that will last forever. He wants to lead us to maturity, verse 4: '. . . so that you may be mature and complete, not lacking anything.' That's not how I feel when I'm going through a hard time, as if I feel I'm not lacking anything. But that's the perspective that James wants us to grasp. But we don't see things that way. James understands that, so he says to us in verse 5, when we're suffering, our biggest need is for wisdom. Verse 5: 'If any of you lacks wisdom, he should ask God who gives generously to all without finding fault, and it will be given to him.' In hardship our greatest need is often for wisdom. It may not seem like it. It usually feels like the greatest need is for a solution to the problem. But James says, 'No, what you actually need most of all is wisdom to face this situation.' We face great pain, great loss, and we just don't know how to respond. We need wisdom. Our lives are full of difficulties and we can't understand where God is in it.

Of course, in the Bible, being wise is not just about being smart. Instead, in the Bible wisdom is about having our understanding and behaviour formed by the recognition of God's sovereignty and holiness. Proverbs says, 'The fear of the Lord is the beginning of wisdom.'. Wisdom is about seeing life from the perspective of the God who is sovereign, in charge and holy, utterly pure. Wisdom isn't about having all the answers. Sometimes the perspective of wisdom is to accept that this awesome, sovereign, transcendent God doesn't have to give us all the answers. But rather than succumbing to easy cynicism, wisdom keeps trusting in the goodness of God, despite the contradictions in our lives. Wisdom sees beyond the suffering to the good and gracious purposes of God; perhaps seeing something of how he is at work in this situation to bring us to maturity and so seeking to respond in faith and obedience. That's what wisdom is about in this context. James says that kind of wisdom is freely available to us if we will but ask. Verse 5: 'If any of you lacks wisdom, he should ask God, who gives generously to all without finding fault, and it will be given to him.' It doesn't mean God will give us the answers to all our questions, but it does mean that he will give us the wisdom that we need to move forward in maturity and faith, if we ask. Wisdom to keep faith in his goodness. Wisdom to begin to see something maybe of his purposes at work in the situation. Wisdom to know how to start responding.

There was one time in my life when I had a particularly dramatic experience of this promise being fulfilled. It was in 1993 and one Saturday morning my wife and I came home from a hospital in Nottingham, having held our two-week-old baby as he took his last few breaths and died. We arrived home and collapsed in a heap at the bottom of the stairs, not really knowing where to put ourselves. Soon after, the telephone rang. Steve from our house group was on the phone. He didn't know what had happened, but in his quiet time that morning he had been reading some words that he felt he had to pass on to us. They were the words drawn from the beginning of 2 Corinthians 1, where Paul says, 'Praise be to the God and Father of our Lord Jesus Christ, the Father of compassion and the God of all comfort, who comforts us in all our troubles, so that we can comfort others with the comfort we ourselves have received from God.' Did that answer all my questions? No. It didn't. There were still many unanswered questions. But, you see, it gave me wisdom from the Lord. Wisdom to have some understanding, even if it's limited, of what God was doing. This pain would not be lost, it would not be wasted. There was purpose. God was there. God is sovereign. He's still holy, he's still good. He's still working out his purposes. We can trust him.

Then James, rather perplexingly, seems to put a condition on this promise. He says, yes, there's wisdom for the asking, verse 5, but verse 6, when we ask, we 'must believe and not doubt, because he who doubts is like a wave of the sea, blown and tossed by the wind. That man should not think he'll receive anything from the Lord; he is a double-minded man, unstable in all he does.'

We're back to our theme of double-mindedness, but now in the context of hardship in the tough places of life, when our values are tested. What's James saying? That if when we're suffering and have doubts, God won't answer? No, God gives graciously to all, without finding fault. And suffering often does lead us to questioning. That's normal. But we can ask those questions in two different ways. We might say: 'Lord, I've trusted you all these years. I've had a quiet time every day. I've tired myself out working for the church and now you let this happen? What do you think you're doing? If this doesn't get sorted out, I'm not going to believe in you any more.' As if our small doubts could threaten God's very existence. In this context, double-mindedness is saying that we will trust God only on our terms, if he delivers what we're asking. But you can't make deals with God like that. He's too big and we're too small. Once you start down that path, you lose all your moorings. You become unstable, unable to receive anything from the Lord, James says, verse 8.

But there is a way of questioning God that actually expresses faith. Maybe it goes something like this: 'Lord, why have you allowed me to experience this pain? What is your purpose in the middle of this? I will not accuse you of evil, or turn from you in the darkness, but please God, I don't understand. Would you please give me wisdom to know what you're doing and to know how you want me to respond.' That's the questioning that expresses faith. To such a request God promises to respond. The reality is, of course, hardship will either send us to God, or drive us from him.

My appeal to you this evening, if you're in tough circumstances, is to resist the temptation to a kind of double-mindedness that puts conditions on our trust of God and instead to turn and run into his arms. Let your tears fall on his shoulders and seek his wisdom to lead you forwards.

Anyone involved in any kind of pastoral ministry will from time to time have to face the pain of seeing Christian people falling foul of the pitfalls and hazards that face us in our Christian discipleship. It's painful, but it happens. Sometimes it happens in quite public or large, dramatic ways. As I was preparing for this evening, I tried to think back to a few of the situations that I found myself involved with over the years. And on reflection, in most of the cases where people have fallen foul of those pitfalls in their Christian discipleship, one of three things had happened. Either they had simply run out of steam in their commitment. They had become weary of the Christian life and gone in search of something easier. Or, they'd allowed themselves to be driven by the longing to satisfy the unbridled human desires and so they'd made a mess sexually or they'd just been overtaken by materialism. They loved the world. Or something awful had happened in their lives and in bitterness of spirit they had turned their backs on God. I'm sure there are other pitfalls and hazards as well, but it seems to me in my experience a lot of the struggles that we face fall into those three experiences. You can live with double-mindedness in the Christian life for so long but if it remains unchallenged, in the end it will undermine our Christian discipleship and cause us to trip up.

I began by telling you about that morning on the platform of my local railway station reflecting on double-mindedness. Those reflections only lasted for a few minutes. I found myself on the train to Cheltenham sitting next to an exceedingly talkative kind of passenger. He talked and talked all the way to Birmingham, when he got off. Life's like that; full of voices, full of clamour so that important voices, important questions get drowned out. That's why I need moments like this, when the other voices are not heard. Moments to be quiet. Moments to allow the sharp words of Scripture to sink into my heart, to expose my double-mindedness and to begin to reshape me. For some, the challenge is to repent of double-mindedness that's crept in and to renew our commitment. For some, the reality is that double-mindedness has already done its work. You've fallen and your Christian discipleship is in a mess. For you, the good news is that the gospel is good news for sinners. This is an evening not to wallow, but to come home and to know God again.

Discipleship Isn't For Loners
by Elaine Duncan

ELAINE DUNCAN

After studying for a psychology degree, followed by a brief spell on the nursing team of a psychiatric unit, Elaine worked for UCCF for fourteen years before moving to Glasgow to work for Scripture Union Scotland as Regional Activities Director. The focus of Elaine's work has always been the gospel amongst young people. One of her greatest joys is to see people (of any age!) gain a fresh insight about God through his word and to grow in their relationship with him. Elaine particularly loves savouring the beauty of God's creation, and walking up the hills of the Lake District and Scotland is her favourite way of enjoying it! Elaine is a Trustee of the Keswick Convention.

Discipleship Isn't For Loners

Introduction

1 John 4 verses 7–21.

Dear friends, let us continue to love one another for love comes from God. Anyone who loves is born of God and knows God, but anyone who does not love does not know God, for God is love. God showed how much he loved us by sending his only Son into the world so that we might have eternal life through him. This is real love. It is not that we loved God, but that he loved us and sent his Son as a sacrifice to take away our sins. Dear friends, since God loved us that much we surely ought to love one another. No-one has ever seen God, but if we love each other God lives in us, and his love has been brought to full expression through us. And God has given us his Spirit as proof that we live in him and he in us. Furthermore, we have seen with our own eyes and now testify that the Father sent his Son to be the Saviour of the world. All who proclaim that Jesus is the Son of God have God living in them and they live in God. We know how much God loves us and we have put our trust in him. God is love, and all who live in love live in God and God lives in them. And as we live in God our love grows more perfect. So we will not be afraid on the day of judgement, but we can face him with confidence because we are like Christ in this world. Such love has no fear, because perfect love expels all fear. If we are afraid it is for fear of judgement, and this shows that his love has not been perfected in us. We love each other as a result of his loving us first. If someone says 'I love God' but hates a Christian brother or sister that person is a liar. For if we don't love people we can see how can we love God who we have not seen. And God himself has commanded us that we must love not only him but our Christian brothers and sisters too.

I want to start tonight by asking you two questions. The first one is how do you think the UK will be won for Christ? It may be that you don't live in the United Kingdom. Well you just replace where you live instead of the UK. The second question is 'How can I be sure I'm a Christian? You may think that these are two quite bizarre questions to start our evening on Christian community. But the interesting thing is that I think the apostle John would give exactly the same answer to both questions.

The importance of love

His answer would be that love that you and I have for fellow believers is key in the answer to these two questions. John writes his first letter to Christians who need to be reassured that they truly are Christians. There are people about in the first century who are teaching things that are tempting them away from Christ. John says to his readers of his first letter, 'There are three tests that you can do to reassure yourself that you are a Christian.' John Stott describes these as the doctrinal test, the moral test and the social test.

The doctrinal test

What the apostle John is saying to these early believers is that you can check if you are a Christian, you can be reassured if you are a Christian first of all by asking yourself 'What do I believe?' There are certain things that Christians believe.

The moral test

We can also reassure ourselves that we are Christians by looking at our behaviour. There are certain ways that Christians will behave.

The social test

We can be reassured that we are Christians by looking at the extent of our belonging together, the depth of our love for one another as Christians. Tonight we want to focus on this area of our relationships together. It is very important because in 1 John chapter 4 verse 12 it says 'No-one has ever seen God, but if we love each other God lives in us, and his love has been brought to full expression through us.' So not only is our love for one another a test and a reassurance that we do actually belong to Christ and we are Christians, but actually John says the world will see the full expression of God's love through our love for one another. That's quite a responsibility.

How will a nation be won for Christ?

What went through your mind when I said 'How will the UK, or whichever country you are from, be won for Christ?' Here in the UK we might have come up with something like *Alpha*. *Alpha* is great, and important in helping people come to a better understanding of who Christ is. What about *Christianity Explored,* another way in which people have their eyes opened to see who Christ is? What about the work that Mark Greene is doing in encouraging us to be witnesses for Christ in our workplace? All these things are important and I believe will be used by God, but there is a more fundamental issue, and it is actually to do with the quality of our relationships within our churches in our Christian communities.

Now relationships are funny things aren't they? You either love them or you hate them. It seems to me that relationships are the greatest source of joy. The times when we experience deep joy, that we are just glad to be human is usually as a result of something within a relationship. But equally relationships are the source of the deepest hurt and pain that we will ever experience. So we have a bit of a love/hate relationship with relationships, don't we?

How do we love one another?

What we learn from the passage in 1 John chapter 4 is that love deals in truth. Read verse 10, 'This is real love. It's not that we loved God, but that he loved us and sent his Son as a sacrifice to take away our sins.' This verse is saying that God has dealt with us in the reality of our sin. Our sin is not something that God pretends isn't there. It's not something that he is happy just to sweep under the carpet. He deals with the reality of it, and that is why Jesus had to come, and die in our place to deal with our sin, all that separates us from the living God. God deals with the reality of who we are. I think we prefer not to do this with one another. We actually prefer to live a pretence with one another. We don't find it too comfortable to face up to who we are with one another and we find in our churches particularly that very often there is a veneer of respectability that goes up as soon as we walk into church. We have barriers between ourselves because we don't like to deal with the reality of who we are. We end up living a pretence. I think we need to learn from how God deals with us. We need to learn how to deal with one another. We need to start being able to face the reality of who one another is, and we need to start to allow people to deal with the reality of who we are. Not just a public face, and a veneer that we put on, but the real us. We need to start relating to one another at a real level. Some of us want to deal in truth but not in love. This is particularly true in the evangelical church where we are really passionate, and rightly so, about doctrinal purity. But very often in our passion and zeal for doctrinal purity we lay love on one side, and we don't focus on the doctrine of unity that is so strongly taught through Scripture. So just as God deals with us in truth and God is love, and love deals in truth, we need to be careful that we don't want to deal in truth without love. It has to be both.

Love involves sacrifice

If we look at verse 10 again we find that God has sent his Son as a sacrifice to take away sin. Jesus is our pattern for how we are to love one another. Loving one another will involve sacrifice. Jesus gave up his own life for us, and you and I need to learn more and more about what it means to give up something of our lives for one another. We need to learn the hard lessons of putting others first, of having their needs and desires first and foremost before our own. That is a real sacrifice.

I want you to notice in this sacrifice that God takes the initiative with us. God hasn't left us with this huge problem of sin, to try and work out how we fix it on our own. God takes the initiative in restoring our relationship with him. Which relationship, at the moment, do you need to take some initiative in? Think about your relationships back at home, your relationships in your local church, maybe even your relationships with somebody that you are here with tonight. But in which relationship are you holding back, waiting for the other person to make the first move? Our God did not do that. He stepped out and reached out towards us, and took the initiative. For how many of us is there a relationship where we need tonight to resolve to take the initiative? It may be a relationship that has broken down for some reason. Alienation has happened, and you are blowed if you're going to make the first move. I wonder if God is saying tonight 'Go on, follow me, take the initiative, you make the first move.'

It's perhaps a relationship that needs to begin to go into a deeper level. It's stuck as a superficial relationship and needs to go deeper. Are you going to be willing to take the initiative in that? How many of us think of so many good things that we could do in some of our relationships? You know, you think about a card that you would like to send somebody, and in fact you write it in your head. You think about the phone call that you know you ought to make, and you have the conversation in your head. You think about that e-mail that you ought to send to someone, and again you write it in your head. But we don't ever quite get to the point of writing it on the card, picking up the phone, pressing the 'send' button on the e-mail. John says to these early Christians in Chapter 3 and verse 18, 'Dear children, let us stop just saying we love each other. Let us show it by our actions.' To take the action is where the sacrifice kicks in. Thinking it in your head, it's a start, but it has to be followed through on into action, and that's where many of us will experience the sacrifice.

Love flows from the security of being loved

Verses 16–18

> God is love and all who live in love live in God and God lives in them. As we live in God our love grows more perfect so we will not be afraid on the day of judgement but we can face him with confidence because we are like Christ here in this world. Such love has no fear because perfect love expels all fear. If we are afraid it is for fear of judgement, and this shows that his love has not been perfected in us.

Our ability to love always flows out of our sense of security. John is saying that God knows the absolute worst about us, and still he loves us. He has done everything that is needed for us to be able to face him on judgement day and not be banished from his presence. He has done everything in Christ dying for you and I on the cross. That means that we will be able to stand before God on judgement day with our heads held high, not with a confidence in ourselves, but a confidence in Christ who has died for us and paid the price. And his righteousness is what God will see as we stand before him.

I think that what John is saying here is 'Look, if you were to think about what is the most fearful thing in life, if you were to think of the thing that would make you the most afraid, then actually it is the judgement of God that says "Go from my presence, I cannot accept you."' That is the most fearful thing in the whole of life that we could face, and John is saying 'God has fixed that. God's love has banished that fear from your heart and mind. He knows the absolute worst about us, and still accepts us because of what Christ has done.' That makes us the most secure people on earth, because that fear is dealt with. We find ourselves afraid and tentative in many relationships, because we think we'll be rejected. We're not confident about somebody getting close to us, and getting to know who we are, because we think 'When they know what I'm really like then they won't want to be with me, they won't want to be my friend. This relationship will just dissolve because they see me for who I am.' But God does know, and he loves us, and you and I can base our love for others on the absolute security of knowing that God loves us.

How do we do all this in day-to-day life? Now I need you to think about relationships that you are in as we go through this next bit, because otherwise it's just theory. We can all sit there and nod and say 'very wise, very wise. Yes I agree with that' and we go home on Saturday and in fact for most of us it probably won't even take until Saturday, and it doesn't make any difference. We want to earth this so that we are actually different and living out a life of love in all our relationships, and particularly with our brothers and sisters in Christ. So we are going to run through a very quick short course in human relationships. This is not my own work, and I don't know who to acknowledge to say thank you for it, but I heard this a few years ago and we have regularly used it in Scripture Union Scotland in some of our training events for young leaders. It's called *A Short Course in Human Relationships*, and tonight I'm just having to claim Holy Spirit copyright because I don't know who to acknowledge for it. And it goes through the seven most important words and then the six most important words and five most important words... I think these will help us if we think about them in relation to particular people in our relationships with one another.

I'm among you as one who serves

This is us, not necessarily speaking these words, but certainly having these words in our mind as an attitude in which we go into relationships. It is the attitude that our Lord Jesus Christ had. He came as a servant, and if you and I are willing to have this attitude with one another, that we serve one another and put the other's interest first, then our relationships will begin to be transformed. We will go into a situation not wanting to be top dog. Now the friend that I live with has got a dog, and at the moment she is looking after a friend's dog as well, and I had two texts this morning telling me of fights that these two dogs are having. It's basically because they don't know whose territory they're on and they're trying to sort out who is top dog, and it's quite messy. I think an ear has been affected. But if you and I go into situations with the attitude that we want to be top dog, then we will bite and devour one another. But if we go in with the attitude that I am among you as one who serves, what a difference that would make in our relationships.

I'm sorry, I made a mistake

One of the things that you and I as human beings find so hard to do is apologise. It's our pride; it gets in the way because we like to think that actually we're OK and we don't make mistakes. We don't like to admit our weakness. I don't know about you but I make mistakes all the time; what I need to learn is to admit it. I'm going to be honest about my failure.

You did a good job

I am going to notice good things, and I'm going to encourage others in the good things that they are doing. Our churches are full of people who feel unappreciated, who are beavering away on all sorts of jobs; the background tasks that have to be done in order for life together to happen, and nobody notices. Will we begin to notice and say, you did a good job?

What do you think?

My opinion is not the only thing that matters, but I don't always remember that. 'What do you think?' We need to learn to refer to one another, and to listen to one another's opinions, and to allow God to use the different opinions and to shape our thinking to be more in line with his thinking. If we think our opinion is the most important, then actually we are trying to take God's place.

I love you

It seems to me in relationships today we can never say this often enough. Our world is crying out for love. It thinks it's crying out for sex, but it's not, it's crying out for love. And in our churches we need to be displaying that love, and actually telling one another that 'I love you.'

Thank you

Be grateful and express appreciation. It builds on the 'You did a good job.' Notice things and express appreciation. As you say 'Thank you' it actually does something inside you. It prevents you and protects you from becoming bitter and becoming cynical, and so it's important to say 'Thank you'.

We

We are in this together. When we come to know Christ we don't just enter into a new vertical relationship with the living God, but we enter into a new horizontal relationship with one another. Now my dad is in this tent tonight, and I love him, and we are bound by a blood tie. We are closely connected, relating to one another with a blood tie. But friends, for all of you here who know Christ and love Christ, then you are my brothers and sisters, and we are tied together with a blood tie that is Christ's himself. Christ's blood binds us together, and that is stronger than any human family relationship. And I believe that within our churches and within our Christian communities, in our workplace, in our neighbourhoods, we need to begin to experience and express this sort of love and commitment for one another.

Our love reflects God's love

It is so important because our love for one another shows God's love to the world. Verse 12 again. 'No-one has ever seen God, but if we love each other God lives in us, and his love has been brought to full expression through us.' John also records the words of Jesus in John 13 verses 34 and 35, which say Jesus says to his disciples 'I am giving you a new commandment. Love each other. Your love for one another will prove to the world that you are my disciples.' How will other people come to know Christ as their Saviour? By the love that we have one for another. How do we know that we are truly Christian? By the love that we have one for another. Friends, let us love one another.

How To Change Your Community For Christ

by Steve Chalke

STEVE CHALKE

Steve Chalke founded Oasis Trust, a Christian charity, in 1985. Initially he set up a hostel for homeless young people in Peckham, south London. Eighteen years on, Oasis Trust has a team of over three hundred staff, students and volunteers, developing and running educational, healthcare and housing initiatives both in the UK and in sixteen other countries on six continents. Steve is the author of twenty-six books, and regularly presents for both ITV and BBC and contributes to Radio 1, 2, 4 and 5 Live. In 1999, Steve initiated a new charity 'Parentalk', inspiring and resourcing parents to enjoy parenthood. He is also the Founding Director of Faithworks – a movement committed to acting as an agent for change by promoting Christian values within our society. Steve was ordained as a Baptist minister in 1981 and was a local minister for four years before setting up Oasis Trust. He lives in south London with his wife Cornelia and their four children.

How To Change Your Community For Christ

Introduction

It's great for me to be at Keswick for all sorts of reasons. One reason it's great for me to be here is because I live in Croydon. I've lived in Croydon for practically all my life. I've been away for little bits, but Croydon is where I was born and brought up and it's where I live now.

What we're going to be talking about is our towns, and our villages, or the cities from which we come, and how the church fulfils its role right at the hub of those communities. In Croydon a year and a bit ago when they had the local elections, the local council put up a banner everywhere. It was designed to get people to vote in the local election. This is what it said: 'Question: What takes just two minutes but lasts four years?' 'Answer: Your vote.' I could not believe that Croydon Council had come up with what had to be such a misguided concept. The reality is that our villages, our towns, our cities become what we vote for; not just once every four years with a tick in somebody else's box so that we leave them responsible whilst we do something else. What we have to do is vote every day of our lives for our community, and the church has got to be, should be, right at the hub of all of that.

Why change your community?

The seminar this morning is entitled 'How to change your community', but first of all I'd like to spend a bit of time looking at 'why'. If
we just do the 'how' but not the 'why' we might be misguided. Just
because there is an opportunity to do something you shouldn't necessarily grasp it and take it. So before we talk about how to engage
ourselves more fully at the hub of our community we need to ask
'Why do we do this?' It could all be a giant sidetrack from the gospel.
There are those in the church who would say that it's taking our eye
off the ball if we engage too much. We are there to preach Christ and
preach Christ crucified not, as someone put it to me a few years ago,
to mess about doing social work. Why do we get involved? I would
say there are two reasons, one to do with society and one to do with
the Bible. I should perhaps take them the other way and talk about
the Bible first, because that's the beginning of the why, but I'd just like
to talk about society to begin with.

The state of society

I read an article in *The Times* and it simply said that Westminster City
Council – Oasis works right in the heart of London – have decided
that they are going to make it illegal to sleep in a shop doorway or in
a sleeping bag anywhere in Westminster. The reality is however that at
Oasis we run a primary care health centre just on the edge of
Westminster. It's London's biggest primary healthcare centre for the
homeless population. We've been running for ten to twelve years. Last
year was our peak year: we did thirteen thousand treatments for
London's homeless population. So at the same time as Westminster
local council are saying there's no reason for people to be homeless in
the twenty-first century, which is what *The Times* said this morning,
we treated thirteen thousand people. And we receive not a penny of
government funding for that project. They say 'There are no homeless.' We say 'But we treated thirteen thousand of these people who
aren't homeless.'

The truth is our society is in a mess. I don't know where you
come from, but I do know this – put your hand up and tell me if

I'm wrong. In your community there are a lack of facilities for young people, kids stand around on street corners, youth crime is rising, teenage pregnancy rates are rising, there are endless sixteen year old lads who leave school without five GCSEs A to C grade. In your community there is unemployment, family breakdown, the problem of the elderly who are alone, problems about healthcare, questions about places you can sit down and be listened to and talk. In your community there are questions about education, about street crime. All of those things are true about your communities. The reason is that around the UK the social infrastructure is unravelling. You could stand the Prime Minister and the Deputy Prime Minister up here and they would both agree. You could get the leader of the opposition to agree.

We live in a country were community is breaking down, fast. Depending on whether you belong to the red team or the blue team, Labour or the Conservatives, you have different words to describe this. If you're part of the red team you talk about building social cohesion and creating community champions, and you talk about something they have in the Home Office called the Active Community Unit. It is understood that you cannot build a community just through money. You need social capital, community champions, social entrepreneurs, people who will make a difference, people who will glue a community together. You can only build a community around the community that gets involved and cares. The reality is that much money and thought and effort is being pushed into how you rebuild the infrastructure of our country. I had breakfast with the Chancellor of the Exchequer, Gordon Brown, to talk about these things last year and he said to me 'Steve, we just cannot find the mechanism,' and he wasn't just talking about the Labour Party, he was talking about the whole political system. 'We cannot find the mechanism that will engage people on the ground so that some of these great needs are met.'

The Commissioner of the Metropolitan Police Force, Sir John Stevens is a Christian. I had lunch with Sir John, and he said 'Steve, I'm a civil servant at the end of the day. I will vote for all the crime busting measures that are put forward.' Stop and search, name and shame, instant fines, more surveillance cameras, longer sentences, more places in security wings: 'I'll vote for all of those things', he said 'because I'm a civil servant and they are all important because they are all dealing with the symptoms.' But he said: 'We know that all the time a gang of young people stand on a street corner, and their only sense of identity, their only sense of belonging comes to them through that gang, and that gang take drugs, gets pregnant, steals mobile phones, they will do those things; and until we provide them with an alternative sense of community we give them nothing. We must not stand there and "tut tut tut". We have to give them community.' That's the task of the church. When Jesus said 'I will build my church, we all know what he was talking about. 'I will build a community of God's people who understand *shalom*, God's Kingdom, my way. I will build that community where the have-nots are now haves, where the excluded are now included.' That is the task of the church. It is what we are called to, to move from the inside to the outside. There is this glorious opportunity here, an open doorway.

If the church has been the Cinderella of welfare care and community development (and we have been), still we have a glorious history. Schools, colleges, universities, medical care, the battle against slavery, the church was there. But we have been driven out. The church used to be the hub of every town. Many of you go to parish churches which physically still are. The church used to be the education centre and the social centre, in the market square, the spiritual centre catering for the whole of life, but our society drove us to the edges. Christianity was old-fashioned. In a new, modern, scientific world it was not wanted any more. It's time for us to get back in the hub of the community. If the church has been the Cinderella of holistic integrated care at the hub of the community, Cinderella has now been invited to the ball. The only question is have we got the courage to leave our sculleries and go? Because some of our sculleries are very well decorated now. They've got comfortable seating in, we've got power point projection, bookstalls, coffee areas. Our sculleries are nice places to hang round in, but we were made to be out there, not in here.

The biblical background

I'd like to read to you from Luke's Gospel chapter 4 verse 14.

> Jesus returned to Galilee in the power of the Spirit. The news about
> him spread throughout the whole countryside. He taught in their syn-
> agogues and everyone praised him. He went to Nazareth where he had
> been brought up, and on the Sabbath day he went, as was his custom,
> to the synagogue and he stood up to read. The scroll of the prophet
> Isaiah was handed to him. Unrolling it, he found the place where it is
> written 'The Spirit of the Lord is upon me because he has anointed
> me to preach good news to the poor and he has sent me to proclaim
> freedom for the prisoners and recovery of sight to the blind; to release
> the oppressed and proclaim the year of the Lord's favour.'

Now when Jesus travelled around the synagogues; what were these
synagogues? What did they look like? Did they look like your parish
church, or your Methodist church? Did they have dry rot in? I can tell
you they were all brand new buildings. There were no old ones. How
do I know? It's quite simple. What were synagogues? Synagogues were
places where Jews worshipped. We go to a church, if I'd have been a
Jew I'd have gone to a synagogue. Christians worship in churches,
Jews worship in synagogues. They used to go on Saturday, we go on
Sunday. That's the deal.

The truth is that Jews didn't worship in synagogues traditionally at
all. In fact there are no synagogues in the whole of the Old Testament;
this is the first chronological mention of the term 'synagogue' in the
Bible, when Jesus went and preached in them. There is not one synagogue in the Old Testament. Synagogues did not exist, Jews did not
worship in synagogues, they had not been invented. That's how we
know that these synagogues Jesus wandered around were relatively
new, because it was a new movement, the synagogue movement.

So the question is, 'If Jews didn't worship in the synagogue, where
did they worship in the Old Testament?' 'In the Temple.' That's a good
answer: however, it's not right. Of course they did worship in the
Temple, but the Temple was a bit like Keswick; you showed up once

a year. The Temple in Jerusalem was somewhere where Jews went on high days and holidays. The place where the Jews worshipped was in the home, and that's where the first churches were. They weren't in buildings. They met in homes and then out into the community. Our buildings are a great blessing and they're a great curse as well, aren't they? We tend to get used to the scullery, and we like the scullery, but we were never meant to live there, just to re-equip ourselves there, to eat there, to get out.

Anyway, Jews worshipped in the home. But when we say that we have to remember two things about the dysfunctionality of our culture. We have two problems and they both coincide with this sentence 'Jews worship in the home.' We have a dysfunctionality about the concept of worship, and we have a dysfunctionality about the concept of home. Apart from that we understand the sentence perfectly well!

Worship

Worship for a Jew was everything (Ps. 24:1). Worship was singing, praying and Bible reading, but it was also partying, eating, laughing, loving, gardening, washing up and farming. Worship was about an attitude of life, not just the formal cultic bits, but we have made it almost just those bits. We are dualists, to give the right term to it. There are two guys in our church. One is an accountant and the other is an accountant. One works for Tear Fund in Nairobi in Kenya, so we pray for him every week and we've got his picture on the board because he's a missionary. The other one is an accountant for Croydon Council. Nobody even knows what he does. He says 'I'm an accountant.' They all go 'zzzzzz'. These two guys are doing the same thing, and they're both doing it for the kingdom of God, both serving Christ full time. But we've divided the world up into those bits and pieces and we've made worship some things that happen on a Sunday morning. But Jews saw their whole life as worship. One of my friends is the Chief Rabbi, Jonathan Sacks, who is a very lovely gentle kind man. 'Steve,' he said, 'I had some of your dysfunctional Christian friends around. We were talking about the Sabbath meal, and they asked me when we did the worship. I was quite taken aback by it. Then I remembered they were dysfunctional Christians, and I knew what to say. "Oh, you mean the prayers and the songs. We do those at the end and this is what they are." They went away happy and ignorant.'

You see, the meal is worship. The cooking is an offering to God, the eating of it together is worship, throwing arms around one another is worship, the drinking of the wine is worship. The laughter is worship, the being with family is worship, the praying is worship, the reading is worship, the singing is worship. A life offered to God is worship and the Jews had that understanding of worship which Paul also understood. You know Romans, 'Present your whole body to Christ as worship'.

Home

Jews worshipped in the home. We also have a wrong view of home because we almost believe that it was probably Jesus who said 'An Englishman's home is his castle.' You can only come when invited for a meal, at a pre-arranged time, but don't come knocking on my door when I'm not expecting you, because we live privatised lives. But the home for Jews was extended, multigenerational and inclusive. The family was higgledy-piggledy. You know that saying where the prophets cry out on God's behalf and they say to the Jews, 'Take care of the widow, the orphan and the refugee.' Now why is that? It is there because, for different reasons, those three categories of people, the widow, the orphan and the refugee, could fall through the safety net of care in Jewish community, which was the family. So God screams 'Get them back in, don't drop them!' Jewish families were big, inclusive, multigenerational and they were the safety net of society.

So the home became for everyone the social centre, the medical centre, the education centre, the job plan, the retirement plan. The home was the hub and the family was what we call extended. By the way, you know we talk about extended family? That is western arrogance. It is part of our colonialism. We shrunk the family. We look back at the South American, or the Asian or the African family, which is much bigger than our family, and so we have to say that's extended, because we haven't got the courage to say our family life is shrivelled. We cannot admit that we have reduced family life, so we have to say they've extended it. We've shrunk it to be unworkable.

In our society we have social services, the Welfare State which is supposed to be the safety net, but the mesh in the Welfare State is too big and lots of people are dropping through. It's failing. What was the synagogue? It was the worship centre. But by worship the Jews meant the singing centre, the sermon centre, the job centre, the education centre. In fact our word school is derived from the root 'synagogue'. But you say 'Oh, that's synagogue, but you've still got the jump to churches.' Well of course, if you read the Acts of the Apostles . . . I was taught in Sunday school that Peter, James and John started lots of churches, but they didn't actually start churches at all. They began Messianic synagogues. They were still Jews. They believed however that the Messiah had come. Their concept of church was of the synagogue, which is why the first big battle in the church in Jerusalem is when they can't feed the Greek widows, and the Greek widows come and complain. What do the apostles do? Do they say 'I'm sorry, you want the synagogue down the road, they're the ones who are supposed to take care of the widows, the orphans and the refugees? We're the church, we do souls'? They say 'No, you're right. Let's appoint seven new leaders.' Interestingly enough, it doesn't even say they prayed about it. I'm sure they did but the important thing in the story is that they made an administrative, strategic and organisational decision that they had the wrong infrastructure in place and that they needed a better infrastructure to meet the needs.

How do you engage your community?

Firstly, know what's actually happening. I go into a lot of churches to speak, as you can imagine and sometimes I go into a church and I meet with the elders or the deacons or the vicars, before a service, and they stand around and they pray. Let me give you a typical prayer. 'We pray that you will move mightily in this community and you will pour out your Spirit and your blessing will come down and there will be a mighty revival and the fire from heaven will fall.' The phrases change depending on denomination and where you are standing but you get the sentiment. 'You will pour down your Spirit and there will be a turning to you and a conversion of the masses. Oh, save souls.' I used to be very impressed by all of that. I now see through it. When I listen to people pray like that, you know what I think? I have to be honest, I think 'These people don't have a clue what they're doing. They have not thought about it, they've not engaged their brain, there's not the foggiest chance, the slightest chance this church is going to grow until this bunch either wise up or ship out, and somebody else with a little bit more commitment and probably a little less blab, gets at the helm.'

I've realised because I know it myself. If I'm talking to somebody and I'm tired at the end and they say 'Would you pray for me, Steve?' I suddenly think 'Argh . . .' so I do one of those general prayers. I put my hand on their shoulder, I just check whether it's a man or a woman, and I say 'Lord, please bless this sister, please fulfil her dreams, work in her life. Let her know your closeness, be with her in her needs, meet her needs...' etc., etc. What I've not given away is 1) I couldn't remember their name, 2) I haven't got the foggiest what they were going on about or need, but 3) a general prayer like that covers everything.

The more we plan and engage, the more realistic our prayers become. Here's a realistic prayer. 'Lord we thank you for Tom and for Jake and for the work they've done over the last six months talking to the local council and setting up the reception centre. We are really grateful for the progress that we have made with the asylum seekers' centre. And we pray for Fred and Margaret with the breakfast club they have started in the local school and the relationships they have built with the head teacher there. We ask that you will be with them this morning as they run the breakfast club, and that they will get a good response from the parents, and we pray that as we grow in relationship with these people so they will see something of you in who we are and what we do.' That was a longer prayer, but it was all in English and it was about things that are actually going on.

Research properly!

What we need to do first to engage our communities is to research. You know those community research things that churches do where you get one of those flip charts, one of those A4 charts, and you go around and you do a survey of the community.

You ask people questions and you find out what they want in the community and then the church does that. If you are doing that, you are doing it wrong. Here's a saying that you will know: 'garbage in, garbage out'. Why are MORI and Gallup so good at doing these surveys? Because it's a skill and an art. Ask silly questions, get stupid answers. Put them down in some research, you'll build a project that's going to fail from the start. Here's how to do community research. Talk to the local council, the Education Authority, the police, the Social Services, the health service, the local headmaster. Pull together the statistics that they have. If you talk to those people, on the web and by phone, they will give you so much information about what's going on in the community and what are the needs, how many young people there are, how many girls fall pregnant, how many kids are leaving school without exams, how many kids are playing truant, how many families there are that are on benefit, how many Child Protection Orders there are, how many elderly people there are that do not have proper support. There might not be an information centre, there might be a huge debt problem, there might be a crisis with ethnic groups that don't speak English as a first language.

When you've got that together, then go with your clip board to visit the headmistress or the bobby on the beat, or the lady who runs the corner shop, or interview three people down the street that you have been told has got the worst drugs problem, or whatever it is. Ask their opinions about the statistics. Say 'Local government says that four out of five people in this community are in debt, what do you think about that?' They'll tell you what they think about that. 'There's nowhere for kids to play around here.' They'll tell you about that. Do your research, that's the first thing.

Strategise

Sometimes we think that strategy is not a very godly thing to do. We should just lean on the Spirit. Actually God is a planner. God is a strategist. Before the beginning of time God planned that at the right time he would send his Son into our world. He didn't sit thinking 'Oh, it's all going wrong, we'll have to go into emergency plans now, what should we do?' He doesn't do things that he's not thought through. God planned. Jesus was a strategist. Paul is a strategist. He wants to preach in Rome, he is thwarted in his plan but he is going there and he achieves it. Planning, strategy, that's spiritual. Don't fall into that dualistic worldview that says spiritual is over here and strategy is over there. To strategise is to be a godly person. To strategise and plan also saves time. I have been in leadership long enough to know that if you do all the hard graft of budgeting and planning and thinking through, you save time, you save stress, you save lives, you save relationships, you achieve more. Strategise and plan.

We are just a year away from the beginning of the next election campaign; September 2004 is when it will all kick off. The big issue will be what about the schools, healthcare, our communities, crime or young people? It's a fantastic opportunity for the church to be the church, to become involved. We began this movement, which is called Faithworks and now supplies resources to churches. We are working with just over a thousand churches, helping them build business plans, strategise, think through what they're doing and how they're doing it and making it sustainable and meeting real needs.

Find partners

As you all know, 'Iron sharpens iron'. Diversity brings strength. You have only got to walk into some churches and look at the lousy way they are decorated to realise there is no woman in leadership there. You need strength. Strength is in diversity. Put a bunch of people who are all the same together and you end up with mediocrity. Draw people together who see things differently and you sharpen. We must engage. Who would be partners? Social Services. The Probation Service. The local Education Authority. The local council. Other voluntary organisations and charities. We will grow, and we'll have impact and strength.

Have you read your community strategy? Your council has a community strategy. You were invited as churches to help form it. It is reviewed each year. It is monitored. It is accountable. Every council in England and Wales has to have one of those. By choice all of the councils in Scotland and Northern Ireland have opted in. It's downloadable from a website. You can write to your councillor, you can have a copy by next week. It sets out the priorities and it asks for partnership. The church is invited to the ball. 'Lord show us the needs in our community' and God shouts down 'Read the community strategy. Read the community plan.' 'Lord, but show us, give us some word of prophecy, give us a picture. . . ' 'Read the community strategy.' We've created a parallel universe.

A little Methodist church came to us as Faithworks. We can help you develop a business plan, a strategy, find out about how we can help you. They said 'We're in a little village and we've only got fourteen people in our church and we're all retired and we're all female. And there are no needs in our community because it's very posh.' Which is a misunderstanding, because you know when Jesus talked about poverty, he didn't mean economic poverty alone. It's isolation in any way, and lack of choice. You can be up and out as well as down and out. Anyway, we said 'Read the community strategy.' They came back and said 'We've discovered there is a need here.' It turned out there was a primary school which had appalling SATS levels and they were struggling with truancy. We said 'Do some research.' So they went to the school, they did some research, they talked to the Local Education Authority. They came back and said 'We think we could run a breakfast club.' A breakfast club is this: kids who eat a healthy breakfast will concentrate more, laugh more, play more, be more sociable, fight less. The school provided the Kelloggs, or whatever it was and the kitchen and one teacher. Two ladies from the church ran this breakfast club. Five kids came, then six kids came. It's now up to thirty kids that come each day. Their mums come. Their mums say they're better at home. 'My little Johnny's never been so good. He doesn't fight, he doesn't kick, he goes to bed on time. He's started reading stuff. Oh, it's fantastic.' The school's gone up, the SATS have been better, the teachers are less stressed. The headmistress thinks it's great. All because the church got involved.

But there were those who wouldn't get involved from the group because 'It's not preaching the gospel. We should be preaching the gospel.' The headmistress, who had been a Christian but had dropped out when she got married, says to her husband 'These people are fantastic, our school's changed, my job's easier, the kids are doing better, we're getting more kids through SATS. We'd better go to the church to say thank you.' They go along to the church to say thank you, they love it. They become Christians, they join the church, the church now has sixteen members. And two of them are wage-earners! Revival came when the church got involved. Faithworks exists to help you with that.

Keswick 2003 Tapes, Videos, CDs and Books

Catalogues and price lists of audio tapes of the Keswick Convention platform and seminar ministry, including much that is not included in this book, can be obtained from:

ICC
Silverdale Road
Eastbourne
BN20 7AB
Tel: 01323 643341
Fax: 01323 649240
www.icc.org.uk

Details of videos and CDs of selected sessions can also be obtained from the above address.

Some previous annual Keswick volumes (all published by STL/Authentic Media) can be obtained from:

The Keswick Convention Centre, Skiddaw Street, Keswick, Cumbria, CA12 4BY
Or from your local Christian Bookseller or direct from the publishers, Authentic Media, PO Box 300, Kingstown Broadway, Carlisle, Cumbria CA3 0QS, UK

Keswick 2004

Week One 17 July – 23 July
Week Two 24 July – 30 July
Week Three 31 July – 6 August

The annual Keswick Convention takes place in the heart of the English Lake District, an area of outstanding natural beauty. It offers an unparalleled opportunity for listening to gifted Bible exposition, experiencing fellowship with Christians from all over the world and enjoying the grandeur of God's creation. Each of the three weeks has a series of morning Bible readings, and then a varied programme of seminars and other events throughout the day, with evening meetings that combine worship and teaching. There is also a full programme for children and youth, and a special track for those with learning difficulties will take place in week 2. K2, the interactive track for those aged in their 20s and 30s also takes place in week 2.

Speakers confirmed for Keswick 2004 are: Bible Readings: Alistair Begg of Parkside Church in Cleveland, Ohio for Week 1, Jonathan Lamb of the Langham Partnership for Week 2 and Nigel Lee of the Whitefield Institute, Cambridge for Week 3. Other speakers that have been confirmed so far include Steve Brady, Ian Coffey, Dave Fenton, Ken Gnanakan, Anne Graham Lotz, Peter Maiden, Michael Ramsden, Dave Richards, Rico Tice and Keith White.

For further information please contact:

The Administrator, Keswick Ministries
PO Box 105, Uckfield, East Sussex
TN22 5GY
Tel: 01435 866034
email: info@keswickconvention.org
Website@ www.keswickministries.org